THE
SEARCH

LORNA SIMCOX

The Friends of Israel Gospel Ministry, Inc.
P. O. Box 908, Bellmawr, NJ 08099

THE SEARCH

Lorna B. Simcox

Visit our Web site at *www.foigm.org*.

Dedication

To someone who had seldom written more than ten pages on one subject, writing a book seemed as impossible as scaling Mt. Everest. But my husband, Tom Simcox, believed I could do it. He tirelessly prayed for me, encouraged me, read every page almost as many times as I did, made me rewrite entire chapters, and gently but firmly guided me to the top of the mountain. To him I dedicate the finished product with the hope that my search will enable others to come, at last, to the end of theirs.

Table of Contents

CHAPTER   PAGE

1. "When You're Dead, You're Dead!" 9

2. Thelma 39

3. Paid in Full 63

4. The Big Red Crayon 95

5. Send Someone Else 117

6. Jack and Joan 141

7. The Road Home 159

Chapter One

⊛

"When You're Dead, You're Dead!"

The first time I heard it I was twenty-nine years old. Not that there was anything unusual about being twenty-nine. But I still wonder how I managed to live so long in a country like America without ever having heard anything like it—particularly since I practically grew up in the newspaper business, where you hear just about everything.

It did, indeed, seem pretty farfetched—even more far-fetched than the story I had heard when I was in California, and that one had seriously strained the seams of credibility. While on the West Coast on business one year, I struck up a friendship with a jeweler who told me that every Thursday night, she and some girlfriends got together with a hypnotist. My friend said she had been a princess in another life and knew that detail to be true because, through the miracle of hypnosis, she regularly traveled back in time to visit the magnificence of her previous existence. If I came, she said, the hypnotist would be happy to hypnotize me as well.

"Who knows," she said enthusiastically. "Maybe you were once a queen or something."

Right. Or maybe I was another Sidd Finch and could throw a fastball at 168 miles an hour. Of course, Sidd Finch couldn't really throw a fastball that fast either. But after the April 1, 1985, issue of *Sports Illustrated* hit the newsstands, just about every baseball fan in America was waiting with baited breath for this tall, lanky, 28-year-old French horn-playing Buddhist mystic from Tibet named Hayden (Sidd) Finch to sign a contract with the New York Mets. According to the article, written by George Plimpton, the fervor over the Mets' newest pitching prospect began on March 14 during spring training in St. Petersburg, Florida. That was when Mel Stottelmyre, the pitching coach, asked hitters John Christensen, Dave Cochrane, and Lenny Dykstra to take a couple of swings at some pitches from someone the Mets were considering signing. Sidd Finch then stepped up to the plate and hammered in some balls that registered 150 to 168 miles per hour on a JUGS Supergun II radar gun. It was all pretty hush-hush at first. Even Met owner Nelson Doubleday, wrote Plimpton, was there.

Except that he wasn't there—and for a very good reason. There was no Sidd Finch! He didn't exist. The article turned out to be completely bogus. Plimpton eventually developed a good baseball novel out of it—*The Curious Case of Sidd Finch* (MacMillan). But when the story first ran, everyone believed it.

I marveled at how sincerely my friend believed she had been a princess. She had even read books that articulately and authoritatively expounded on the "truths" of reincarnation. But just because something appeared in print didn't make it so.

Consider, for example, the curious case of the origin of the bathtub. In 1917 noted journalist H. L. Mencken wove a masterpiece of fabrication that has yet to become completely undone.

In one of the most fanciful newspaper hoaxes of all time, Mencken, then a writer for the *New York Evening Mail*, wrote a piece hailing the seventy-fifth anniversary of the bathtub, a convenience that he said came to this country in 1842 thanks to a man named Adam Thompson. Mencken wrote that Thompson had a 7- x 4-foot, 1,750-pound tub installed in his home in Cincinnati and immediately suffered the rebuke of many Americans who vilified the vessel, calling it a variety of names including immoral, elitist, unhealthy, and, of all things, unlawful. Mencken even claimed that bathing finally gained respectability only after President Millard Fillmore had the first bathtub installed in the White House in 1851.[1]

Eight and one-half years later, Mencken confessed that the entire article was pure hooey, but by then his "facts" had made it around the globe and had been reprinted and believed the world over. Even his retraction couldn't retract them. According to an article in *Country Home* magazine, Mencken had had this to say about that:

> *I began to encounter my preposterous "facts" in the writings of other men. They began to be cited by medical men as proof of the progress of public hygiene. . . They were alluded to on the floor of Congress. They crossed the ocean and were discussed solemnly in England and on the continent.*

*I began to find them in standard works of refer-
ence. Today, I believe, they are accepted as gospel
everywhere on Earth.*[2]

Just how much bogus material has actually become
woven into the fabric of everyday life on this earth is anyone's guess. Apparently the weaving is not all that hard to
do; yet the process of separating the truth from the fiction
can often be a tough and painful extraction.

A world-renowned educator once showed a convention
hall filled with teachers how to enable a young student to
get in touch with a "friendly spirit guide" who would help
her learn better. His fans praised and applauded his work;
his detractors said he was using the little girl to channel
demons. Both sides claimed to possess the truth. Obviously,
one side was wrong.

Fiction masquerading as truth may not matter much
when it comes to things like baseball and bathtubs. But
what about when it comes to the weightier matters of life?
Is there reincarnation? Is there a God? Did God create the
world, or did it evolve over billions and billions of years? Is
there life beyond the grave? Who is Jesus, anyway? If there
is a God, what is He like? Does He care about me, and how
can I find Him? These are important issues. What is the
truth? How much fiction concerning these subjects has
wormed its way into the annals of existence so that we
swallow the deception whole without blinking an eye?

Mencken wrote three retractions of his bathtub bunkum,
but to no avail. The die had been cast. The fiction had been
so successfully woven into the fabric of human life that
even Mencken himself couldn't pull it out. Why? "No normal human being," he wrote, "wants to hear the truth. It is
the passion of a small and aberrant minority . . . They are

hated for telling it while they live, and when they die they are swiftly forgotten. What remains in the world . . . is a series of long-tested and solidly agreeable lies."[3]

When I was twenty-nine I knew I had heard the biggest lie of all. I was happily sewing a maternity top for myself on my mother's little black Singer Featherweight when I stopped to listen to a television interview that had captured my attention. First, there was a little talk about Judaism—something I knew a great deal about—then a little more talk about Messiah.

Anxious to hear about that rarely mentioned, almost mystical being who my Hebrew school teacher had said would someday come and right all wrongs done to my people, I temporarily abandoned my machine and strolled over to the television. I gazed expectantly into the face of the pleasant-looking Jewish man being interviewed.

"The Jewish people have been looking for the Messiah for thousands of years, haven't they?" said the program's host.

"Yes," replied the gentleman, "and he has already come."

"What?" I asked aloud, as if someone had been there to answer. "What in the world is he talking about?" The man who had casually piqued my interest suddenly became the object of my intense scrutiny. He was relatively handsome—no bizarre distinguishing characteristics. His dark, wavy hair was stylishly well trimmed; his suit, conservative and tasteful; and his speech, articulate—all of which made me wonder how such a normal-looking Jew could be so grossly misinformed.

"Jesus is the Messiah my people have been looking for all along," he said.

JESUS! JESUS! Of all people! Where in the world did he ever get the idea that Jesus was the Messiah of Israel! Was he NUTS! Was he INSANE! JESUS! Who in the world could possibly believe THAT! In all my twenty-nine years I had never heard anything so preposterous or so utterly detestable.

The man continued to talk, but I had stopped listening. In those brief moments, my surprise had escalated into indignation, then into unbridled outrage. Unwilling to hear another word, I lunged forward, turned off the TV, and banished the now repulsive-looking traitor from my home, screaming over and over at the darkened television set, "You're not fit to call yourself a Jew!"

I had grown up in a Conservative Jewish home. In an age when "dysfunctional" seemed to characterize the average family, mine functioned perfectly. Perhaps it was because family was so important to my parents. Both of them were immigrants who had escaped the long arm of Adolph Hitler. Dad, the middle of eight children, was born on December 19, 1899, in what was then Austria-Hungary. My father had considered himself an Austrian until, one day, he found that Romania had absorbed his part of the world.

According to my Uncle Saul (my father's brother and the only one who ever told me anything about my father's life in Europe), Dad had been exempted from military service to Austria-Hungary because he was severely underweight. But the Romanian army was not so fussy. It dispatched men on horseback who hunted my father down, seized him, and force-marched him for several days all the way back to a location deep in Romania. My uncle chuckled as he told the story, because the intent of the army to do my father harm actually turned out for his good. By the time he arrived at the appointed destination, he was so emaciated and near death that the army rejected him anyway, a move that actually saved his life. If there was one place you did not want to be if you were a Jew, it was the Romanian army.

Romania had no love for the Jewish people. It harshly discriminated against them to the point of even denying them civil rights through Article VII of its 1866 constitution. The article was eventually repealed, but the clause in the 1923 constitution that granted them citizenship provoked such violent hostility among the Gentiles that many Jews outwardly embraced Christianity just to avoid persecution, longing all the while to be able to live like Jews.

I know almost nothing about my father's parents apart from their names and the fact that they both died in Europe. At some point the eldest brother, Itzak, managed to make his way to New York City, where he earned enough money to bring the next eldest brother, Moshe. After Uncle Mo arrived, the two combined forces to finance passage for the third brother. Then came brother number four—Louis, my dad. He arrived with his older sister in 1933. They entered the *Goldina Medina*—the Golden Land, as America was fondly called in Yiddish—through Ellis

Island, sailing into New York Harbor past the Statue of Liberty that bears the immortal words of a Jewish girl named Emma Lazarus, who must have understood something of the melancholy history of her people.

> *Give me your tired, your poor,*
> *Your huddled masses yearning to breathe free*
> *The wretched refuse of your teeming shore.*
> *Send these, the homeless, tempest-tost to me,*
> *I lift my lamp beside the golden door!*

The *Goldina Medina.*   Unfortunately, one of Daddy's brothers and three of his sisters were still yearning to breathe free when America slammed the golden door shut. My father and his sister Anna became the last of the family to enter the United States.   The remaining four made it to Montreal, Canada.

As a skinny, poor, and uneducated European Jew arriving in New York City during the Depression, Dad possessed more hope than he did anything else.   Often he had little to eat.   He painted houses for a living but hated it. Eventually, he settled in Vermont, where he started his own shaving brush-manufacturing company.   Then, in 1947, while visiting my uncle in Montreal, he met my mother. They were married in Montreal in 1948.

Of the wretchedness Daddy left behind in Romania, he said absolutely nothing.   No matter how difficult life was here, it was infinitely better than it was there, particularly for Jews.   He had gratefully become an American with no desire to return to Europe even for a visit—if, indeed, there was anyone left to visit.   When World War II had ended in 1945, Jewish life around the globe was in chaos.   Few Jews knew who among their relatives in Europe had survived the Holocaust or how to find them.

My mother endured for fifteen years not knowing what had befallen her family. Mom was born in the Ukraine in 1915 during the final, turbulent years of Nicholas II, the last czar of Russia and a vicious anti-Semite. Jews, as usual, feared for their lives. Bands of cutthroats routinely descended upon Jewish villages and homes, massacring defenseless Jewish men, women, and children in organized, government-sanctioned killing sprees called *pogroms*. The only time the authorities interfered was to prevent the Jewish people from protecting themselves.

The Bolshevik Revolution in 1917 did not improve things. After the czarist government collapsed, the Bolsheviks took up the mantle of persecution and tried to exterminate the Jews completely. Between 1919 and 1921 there were an estimated 1,200 pogroms in the Ukraine alone.

My mother never knew her parents. Her father was murdered while driving a vegetable wagon to market. Mom was three. Her older brother was about five at the time, and her younger brother was about a year old. My grandmother was so devastated she died a year later, leaving her three children to her parents, whose names I don't know.

Like my father, my mother never talked much about that time in her life apart from expressing her devotion to her brothers, whom she missed terribly. At age sixteen she was persuaded to sail to North America using documents that falsified her age to make her older. Emigrating would preserve her life, she was told. The Communist government refused to release her older brother because he was due to enter the army and contended that her younger brother was too young to leave.

So in 1931, alone and knowing not a word of English, she left behind the only two people in the world who she felt really loved her, and she traveled steerage aboard a ship that brought her to the new world—the city of Montreal, Canada. Her Uncle Akiva, an Orthodox Jewish rabbi, made a home for her with his wife and their four Canadian-born children. They communicated in Yiddish, the universal language of Judaism that spans all oceans, crosses all cultures, and binds together the physical descendants of Jacob.

Homesick for her family in the Ukraine and unspeakably lonely, my mother cried herself to sleep each night on her cot in the kitchen. At some point she went to work in a factory filled with Russian-Jewish immigrants and made friendships that lasted her whole life. Every dime she earned she saved with dreams of bringing her brothers to Montreal. Sometimes she dipped into the nest egg to purchase fabric for suits for them with the dubious assurance that the fabric would make its way to the Soviet Union.

At night she lay on her cot and read for hours by candlelight, trying to master English by devouring books. And master it she did. She learned it so well, in fact, that when she left the factory for a better position as a salesgirl in a department store, she spoke impeccable English with a Canadian accent and was on her way to what would become fluency in French also. But she continued to write in Russian to her brothers. Through their letters, they exchanged bits of their lives. She shared in both their marriages through photographs, and she rejoiced over the births of her older brother's children. In 1942 a photograph arrived of her older brother, his wife and children, and her younger brother with his wife. My mother brought it to a photo studio in Montreal, had an enlargement made, and had her picture inserted in a space that seemed divinely appointed for that very purpose. It was the last communication she would ever receive from any of them. Shortly after the picture was taken, the Nazis arrived.

Soon news began circulating about Nazis herding Jews like cattle into boxcars and incinerating them in ovens. By the time the war ended in 1945, she had no idea who was dead or who was alive.

Around 1958, through relatives who had made it to Israel, my mother learned of her family's fate. Her sisters-in-law, her baby niece and nephew, and her younger brother were all dead. Only her older brother had survived, and she was warned never to contact him because it would mean his certain death. She kept her finest picture of him on our piano all her life and died in 1967 without ever seeing him again.

Because they understood only too well how thin the thread of Jewish life could be, nothing was more important to my parents than my brother and me. They strove to keep our little household secure and often admonished us to "stay close. Keep the family together." They made sure we never doubted their love for us, and they bestowed upon us a wonderful home-life filled with good times, warmth, and tenderness.

My father particularly lavished us with outward shows of love and affection. He even made up little songs for my brother and me that we happily sang with him, and he delighted us with adventurous bedtime stories that usually revolved around his favorite pastime—fishing.

Fishing was never my idea of a good time, but it taught me a lot about my dad. He was a saint with the patience of Job. He could sit contentedly for hours in a little boat on Lake Champlain, surrounded by Vermont countryside. I think it was Daddy's idea of heaven on earth. It sure was not mine. I never understood how thirty minutes of actual fish-catching compensated for the other eight hours of total boredom. But Daddy loved it. He loved the peace and quiet. He loved the fresh air. He loved to fish. He loved living in Vermont. But most of all, he loved having our whole family together.

And he was smart. Given the opportunity to get an education, he could have become an outstanding engineer. He designed almost every machine used in his factory and could duplicate the most complex piece of equipment simply by looking at a picture of it. When homemade go-carts became the rage, he and my brother went to his factory every night after dinner. There they built my brother a go-cart that became the envy of every boy on the block. It was so aerodynamically sound it handily won every race in the neighborhood.

He also played an expert game of chess. He won the regional chess championship every year for almost ten years running, and one year he came within inches of capturing the New England chess championship. Dad didn't talk much about politics, but he made certain of his views well known. He detested the British and Franklin Roosevelt, and he adored Harry S. Truman. I'm convinced that the events of the 1940s forever shaped both my father's politics and his theology. Dad had seen Hitler systematically exterminate two-thirds of European Jewry while the rest of the world—including the United States— looked on, refusing to provide sanctuary. Whereas the U.S. had admitted Jews generously prior to 1933, it accepted only a paltry 200,000 Jewish refugees between 1933 and 1943, when they still could have escaped from Europe, and an open door would have saved millions of lives.[4]

One of the few times I ever saw my father livid was when he told me about President Roosevelt and the voyage of the SS St. Louis. The St. Louis was an oceanliner that had left Germany for Cuba on May 13, 1939, carrying 930 Jewish passengers fleeing the Nazis. When it arrived in Cuba, the government refused to honor the visas and revoked the landing certificates. It cold-bloodedly demanded one million dollars to let the refugees disembark. No country would provide the funds or give the Jewish people sanctuary. Roosevelt refused them entrance into the United States despite repeated appeals, including one from the ship's German captain and another that ran as an editorial in *The New York Times.* In addition, the U.S. Coast Guard patrolled the waters, choking anyone's hope of even swimming to safety. As the ship sailed back to Europe and death, the passengers could see the lights of Miami, Florida, glowing in the distance.[5]

"Give me your tired, your poor, your huddled masses, yearning to breathe free." But the desperate Jews of Europe, nobody wanted. Even today America bears that disgrace. "The refusal of the Western democracies, especially the United States, to give them refuge and shelter is second in infamy only to the slaughter and persecution themselves," writes Abba Eban in his book *Personal Witness, Israel Through My Eyes* (Putnam).[6] For this cause, my father hated Franklin Roosevelt.

He detested the British for much the same reason. By the latter part of its mandate rule of Palestine, the British government bore no resemblance to the Britain that had birthed the Balfour Declaration in November 1917, supporting the establishment of a Jewish national homeland in Palestine. By World War II things had changed drastically. The British government had become so anti-Jewish that it unflinchingly refused to allow Jews fleeing Hitler to enter the Holy Land, even though the Palestinian Arabs were aligned with Germany—Britain's sworn enemy—and the Palestinian Jews were fighting in the British army.

Britain clearly exhibited its bias in 1941 when the *Struma* arrived. The *Struma* was a broken-down ship that had miraculously made its way from Europe to Palestine loaded with Jewish refugees. Rather than give it permission to dock, the British let it sink in the Mediterranean. More than seven hundred people died, including more than three hundred women and children.[7]

After the war ended, Britain appeared even more determined not to let a single person of Jewish blood set foot on the ancient soil. In 1947 the ship *Exodus* arrived at Haifa, bearing 4,500 destitute Jewish men, women, and children who had survived the death camps. Rather than let them enter Palestine, the British used rifle butts, hose pipes, and tear gas to forcibly transfer these concentration camp victims to British prison boats, where they were locked in cages and shipped back to Europe.[8]

My father helplessly looked on. What he saw was a Gentile world that cared nothing for the children of Israel. The Jewish people had groped their way through a crucible of anguish and torture that qualified as one of the darkest commentaries on man's inhumanity to man, only to be further stomped and beaten down in their time of need. Had it not been for one man, in Dad's view, the Jewish people would still be homeless today.

That man, of course, was Harry S. Truman. Against the vitriolic protests of the entire U.S. State Department and the American delegation at the United Nations, both of which were working feverishly to convince the UN to revoke its November 29, 1947, partition of Palestine, Harry Truman bestowed American presidential recognition upon the fledgling Jewish homeland eleven minutes after it declared its statehood on May 14, 1948.[9] That lone act had turned my father into a Truman fan forever. The other events of that decade, however, had turned him into an atheist. If there were a God, Daddy said, He would not have allowed six million Jews to die at the savage hands of the Nazis.

My father's atheism precluded him from encouraging me toward any faith in God. It was, after all, one thing to be a Jew and quite another to be religious. He had sacrificed considerably to send my brother and me to Hebrew school from kindergarten through high school. Yet he refused to attend the synagogue except to take us to the Purim carnival or to see us in a performance there or to cheer us on when we graduated or received an award.

In fact, he never would have joined the synagogue at all had it not been for our family doctor who was the president of the congregation at the time. Where my mother had failed, the doctor was successful in convincing Dad that if he wanted his children to grow up as Jews, they needed a Jewish education. So Daddy joined the *shul* (Yiddish for synagogue) and supported us in everything we did, including the seemingly endless and laborious task of chauffeuring us to and from the place two or three times a day, four and sometimes five days a week, so we could attend classes. And he did it without complaint because he wanted us to understand our Jewish heritage. Jews, he said, had to stick together or they would be annihilated by a hateful, anti-Semitic world. Consequently, my father forbade me to date anyone who wasn't Jewish; and although he loved me as much as any man could possibly love a daughter, he also warned me that if I ever married outside the faith, he would cast me off forever.

His irreligiosity made life somewhat difficult for my mother. Her Uncle Akiva, the Orthodox rabbi, had instructed her diligently in the importance of the traditions of the faith. During her first years of marriage, she lit the Sabbath candles faithfully every Friday night until Dad's scorn became more than she could bear and she quit—but not before teaching me how to do it. She always wanted to attend synagogue during the high holidays (Rosh Hashanah and Yom Kippur), but my father wouldn't purchase the required tickets until the last two years of my mother's agony with cancer. Out of his love for her he relented, and they went together.

Although we held no formal ceremonial observances in our home, Mom was a fabulous cook and treated us to all the traditional goodies that accompanied each Jewish holiday. An immaculate housekeeper, she became even more immaculate at Passover, thoroughly scouring everything to rid our home of leaven in accordance with Jewish law. Although we never kept kosher to the point of maintaining separate sets of dinnerware for milk meals and meat meals, we never *ever* mixed milk with meat, and we maintained separate dinnerware for Passover—my favorite holiday of the year. For eight days we ate nothing containing leaven. I even took peanut butter and jelly sandwiches on matzoh to school for lunch. It wasn't my favorite, but Mom more than made up for it with the marvelous holiday dinners she prepared.

Mealtimes were always fun because we sat around the dining room table and talked, unless, of course, my dad's family was over. Then my brother became the only person I could understand. All the adult conversation switched to Yiddish. How my brother and I failed to conquer that language is beyond me, considering it was all my parents ever spoke to each other. At family get-togethers, my brother and I would head for the television while the aunts and uncles hashed over the smallest to greatest events of life in Yiddish.

At my uncle's home in Montreal, it was Yiddish again; but my brother and I so adored our Uncle Saul that we contented ourselves until he was free to talk to us—in English. The worst afflictions were the dreaded visits with *Mima* and *Fetter* (Yiddish for aunt and uncle). *Fetter* was my mother's dear Uncle Akiva. We had been taught to call them Grandma and Grandpa. They were elderly, gentle, frail-looking old-world people who still lived in the Jewish immigrant section of Montreal. They spoke not a word of English, had no television I could ever locate, and lived in an apartment that seemed as though it had not benefited from an open window since the Bolshevik Revolution. My brother and I would vegetate in their dark, stuffy living room with nothing to do while my parents chatted with them for hours in Yiddish. Fishing was more fun.

Our frequent jaunts to Montreal also involved making the rounds of various kosher butcher shops and fish markets, where we would lay in enough supplies to keep our freezer stocked for months. Kosher meats and other Jewish specialty items were cheaper and easier to find in Montreal.

Cheaper was good. Daddy's business declined steadily in the 1960s. Before it got so bad that she could no longer afford it, my mother bought only kosher meats. Beef came from the kosher butcher shop; but the chickens were another story. For those, she sent my father to the *shochet* (pronounced shoiychet in Yiddish), the only man in town certified to slaughter poultry in the manner prescribed by Jewish law.

Our chickens were certainly the freshest in the neighborhood: they were the only ones with feathers and feet still on them! First Mom would "flick" the chickens, as she called it, removing the feathers. Then she severed the bony, skinny feet and stored them for use later in a recipe with an unpronounceable Yiddish name, a yellowish green appearance, and a taste I have mercifully forgotten. Then she cut the chickens, cleaned the chickens, and soaked the chickens in salt to remove all trace of blood, as dictated by Jewish law.

It devastated her when she finally had to resort to buying *trayf* (non-kosher). She was so ashamed that she would bury the poultry in the bottom of her shopping cart, hoping that no one from the Jewish community would see it.

Rarely was there money for store-bought clothes. Almost everything I wore she made on her little black Singer Featherweight, which she set up on the dining room table. Every sweater I owned she had knitted or had taught me how to knit.

At forty-six, my mother was diagnosed with breast cancer. I was eleven years old. Despite surgery after surgery, she never gave up. I'll never forget the time I outgrew my favorite party dress. There was no money to buy fabric to make another. So she carefully took it apart, redesigned it, recut it, and reassembled it. She added a little scrap of lace here, a little strip of ribbon there, and presented me with the most beautiful dress I had ever seen.

It seemed as though she never slept. At night in bed, I could hear the steady hum of her little machine sewing away downstairs. Every curtain and drapery in the house was made by my mother. She even made my bedspread. She stripped all the floors and woodwork and refinished them. All this she did while wearing a back brace, necessary after a spinal fusion of dubious worth that probably would not even have been performed today.

For six long years she suffered with cancer. The more her condition deteriorated, the more she spoke to me about death. Her outlook was bleak: "I'll be six feet under and that will be the end of it," she would say. But I could tell that she longed for more. Ever the reader, she scrupulously examined books with titles like *Man's Search for Meaning*; but the peace she sought through her heartbreaking illness always managed to elude her. She once summed up the results of all her research with the old Jewish standby: "When you're dead, you're dead."

My mother finally succumbed to cancer in January 1967. I had just turned seventeen. My brother was fourteen. My father was sixty-seven. Her death devastated him. He never really recovered, but he never complained. Some months later the three of us went through her old steamer trunk. It had journeyed with her all the way from the Ukraine those many years ago and now held her most treasured items: old photos of family and friends, family records, my baby book, my brother's baby blanket, her favorite pairs of shoes. . . . For the first time in my life, I saw my father cry.

"There will never be anyone for me but your mother," he told me. And there never was. Mother's death drew us even closer to each other and to my Uncle Saul.

One morning, while Dad with sitting in the kitchen drinking his customary coffee from an old *yahrtzeik** glass, he looked at me and said, "Something's wrong with Saul."

"How do you know that?" I asked. "He's probably fine."

"I just know," he replied. "I haven't heard from him in a few days." Daddy and Uncle Saul usually spoke by telephone every day. So Dad called Montreal and discovered

---

*a glass containing a candle that burns for 24 hours to commemorate the anniversary of the death of a loved one

his brother had suffered a heart attack. My ordinarily composed father was so shaken that he could not even drive. For the first time ever, he boarded a bus to Montreal and nearly collapsed in the hospital when he saw the extent of the paraphernalia wired to my uncle in an effort to keep him alive. From then on, we all feared that my uncle's days were numbered.

Yet in June 1970, it was my father who died. He had lived just long enough to see my brother graduate from high school two weeks earlier. I had completed my junior year at the University of Vermont and had barely arrived in Los Angeles with my friend Nancy to attend the University of California at Los Angeles (UCLA) for the summer. My brother called and we immediately flew home.

My brother picked us up at the airport. Apparently Daddy had suffered a massive stroke. He never regained consciousness. My brother, looking so thin and burdened down, comforted me by reaffirming what we had been taught all our lives. "Lorna, " he said, "we've got to stay close. We've got to always keep the family together."

We buried my father next to my mother in Hebrew Holy Society Cemetery and immediately went to my uncle's home in Montreal where we sat *Shiva* (7-day period of intense mourning). I felt so bad for Uncle Saul. I knew that losing Daddy had shattered him almost as much as it had us. Because of his bad heart, everyone had assumed he would die first, although he was much younger than my father.

Uncle Saul was always special to us. We loved him with the same loyalty with which we had loved my dad. And we knew that he loved us. Many times, through all kinds of weather, we drove to Montreal to see him. Over and over he assured us that he would take care of us as though we were his own; and we knew he meant it.

But that was not to be. About six months after Daddy died, Uncle Saul died in Montreal. As far as my brother and I were concerned, there was no one left. The aunts and uncles remaining on my father's side lived far away and rarely called. It was truly just the two of us now. We were on our own.

Fortunately, Burlington, Vermont, was a small, tightly knit community. We had lived there all our lives and had many good friends. During my freshman year at the University of Vermont, I had started working part-time at the local newspaper, where the managing editor treated me more like a daughter than an employee. He started me out in the back shop setting type and proofreading; but after two years, he moved me into the newsroom, where I began to write.

There I groaned my way through hours of obituaries, fender-benders, and rewrites. The rewrites were the worst. All press releases and copy turned in by correspondents landed in the rewrite basket, to be fished out later and transformed into proper newspaper articles by either a reporter who had nothing to do (which was never) or me. I was certain the odious things bred in captivity. By the end of my first year in the newsroom, I decided that I had descended into rewrite hell.

One night, as I plodded through the basket, a big story broke. The education commissioner had resigned. One of our reporters at the state capital had gotten the story but had not secured all the necessary information; and the deadline for the early edition was fast approaching.

"Lorna," the state editor shouted across the newsroom. "Call up the education commissioner and ask him *blah blah blah*" (he told me what to ask). It was now 11 P.M.—not the friendliest time to be calling people at home. Nor was I the best person for the task. Besides being young and inexperienced, I was extremely timid and unsure of myself. Out of terror, I scrupulously avoided anything that even hinted at public speaking, and I tried desperately to blend into the background everywhere I went. The thought of calling the commissioner of education paralyzed me.

"I can't do that," I shouted back.

"Just do it!"

Reluctantly, I called. I apologized for the lateness of the hour, asked the question, and hung up. Without leaving my desk, I relayed the man's reply to my state editor.

"Well, why didn't you ask him *blah blah blah?*" he shouted back.

"Because you didn't tell me," I said.

"Call him back."

"I can't call him back," I said, thoroughly embarrassed.

"Just call him back, Lorna."

I called back, apologized profusely, asked the question, and hung up. When I gave my editor the response, the next thing I heard was, "Why didn't you ask him . . . " and a new set of *blah blah blahs*. "Call him back."

"No!" I protested. "I won't call him back."

Finally the matter was turned over to a reporter who not only called back but stayed on the phone awhile and turned out a nice little story. "I'll never make a reporter," I thought to myself.

But my editors didn't give up on me. Several months later the state editor got wind of the fact that one of our United States senators was home for the weekend.

"Lorna," he again bellowed across the newsroom. "Call Senator (Robert) Stafford and ask him what he plans to do about *blah blah blah*. Here's his home phone number."

"Isn't there anyone else who can do it?" I protested, desperate to wrangle my way out of it.

"No," he said. "Everyone else is busy."

Determined not to repeat my previous fiasco, I carefully orchestrated my offensive. First, of course, I would introduce myself and state what newspaper I was with. Since we were by far the largest one in the state, I knew he had to speak to me. Then I deliberated at length over the phraseology, rehearsed my little speech and my questions at least ten times, screwed my courage to the sticking place, dialed the telephone number, and waited.

Soon a man answered the phone, and I launched into my well-prepared dissertation. I was quite proud of myself. After I finished, I perched my fingers atop the typewriter keys and got ready to record the senator's response. That's when the voice on the other end of the line replied: "Honey, I'd love to help you, but this is Hargreaves Market."

Hargreaves Market! I was mortified. After all that work it turned out I had dialed the wrong number! When I regained my composure and called again, I mercifully discovered that Senator Stafford was out for the evening. And so began my career in journalism.

In due time, though, I learned my craft. As a general assignment reporter, I covered a smattering of everything: education, lawsuits, labor disputes, prison breaks, press conferences, etc. Eventually I became one of the reporters to fill in at the Capitol Bureau when a statehouse reporter was sick or on vacation. I grew accustomed to dealing with members of the prominent elite as well as the obscure and downtrodden; and I generally knew what was going on even when it wasn't fit to print. It became standard practice to pick up the telephone and get through to whomever I chose; and when I wanted information, I went directly to the source, be it a senator, a commissioner, or a dishwasher.

I also grew accustomed to dealing with death as news. There was death by heart attack, death by drowning, death by fatal car accident, death by suicide. You name it. Murder was the only form I couldn't get used to, but even then I did my job. News was news.

One dark night I almost froze in a blizzard while trying to cover an airplane crash. The area was so remote and the snow so deep that the only way I could reach the site was to inch my way behind the snowplows that were laboriously carving out a path for the police cars and ambulances. Shortly before midnight, I trudged through the snow in search of a telephone to call in the story. I finally found one in a cow barn that I hated to leave because it was warm, dry, and lit. But the story was not in the barn. So after I finished dictating, I went back into the darkness and snow, where I remained until the wee hours of the morning, watching as rescue workers on snowmobiles extracted one body after another from the wreckage and transported them down the slope to the ambulances. The only lights outside were the moon, the stars, and the headlamps on the snowmobiles as they glided up the mountain in search of life, only to return to us with yet another body in a bag. There were no survivors.

As all good editors do, mine saw to it that I was thoroughly schooled in the overriding importance of accuracy and truth. No corroboration—no story. Truth, however, is not always easy to recognize, even when you're looking for it. I once covered a bitter controversy that overtook the state when a group of people calling themselves "born-again" Christians objected to an elementary school social studies curriculum that they claimed taught evolution and genocide. I spent weeks researching the story. I sat in the classroom and observed as the curriculum was being taught. I interviewed children, teachers, superintendents, and school board members across the state. I watched the same films the children watched, talked to a creator of the program at Harvard, and sniffed out every little detail I could in an attempt to write a fair and accurate story.

What resulted was a four-part series that everyone generally considered very well balanced—everyone that is, but the born-again Christians. They were a stubborn and narrow-minded lot, to my way of thinking. For some reason, they felt that I had missed the point of their argument.

Their gravest concern had revolved around the materials that taught the lifestyle of a primitive tribe of Eskimos. These Eskimos routinely left infant girls and old people out on the ice to die because it was simply inexpedient to drag them around from village to village.

"Is your teacher teaching you that it's okay to do this?" I had asked a little blonde-headed boy as I milled around the classroom, questioning students.

"No," he replied.

"Well," I continued, "how do you feel about it?"

"It's just what they do. That's how they live," he said matter-of-factly, accepting the practice of genocide as though it were a simple mathematical equation. Did the material teach that genocide was right? No. And it didn't teach that it was wrong either.

The born-again Christians denounced the curriculum from start to finish. They said it taught secular humanism in a form subtly designed to infiltrate the minds of impressionable youngsters with the intent of eroding the basic moral absolutes of right and wrong. Everyone else said the Christians were nuts.

Interestingly, they were the only people I met the entire time I lived in Vermont who claimed to be "born again." Not that I had the foggiest notion what that meant. I assumed it described Gentiles who had stopped attending church and then, at some point, had decided to give religion a second chance. Although these Christians seemed more intense than most, they never saw fit to explain the terminology; and I assumed that a rose by any other name . . . As far as I was concerned, Jews were born Jewish and Gentiles were born Christian, with the exception of those who were obviously born something else, such as Buddhist, Hindu, Shinto, etc. At this particular meeting we all stuck to the topic of the curriculum, and not once did anyone mention the name of Jesus.

At twenty-six I was promoted to city editor. It didn't take me long to realize that my new position jettisoned almost everything I had enjoyed most about my work. Instead of being out where the action was (covering a story), I was trapped behind a desk; instead of writing my own copy, I was fixing everybody else's; and instead of being responsible for myself, I was responsible for myself and everyone else as well. More than that, though, I was ready to leave Vermont.

Fortunately, it was the 1970s, and the newspaper business was going through an industrial revolution that had been a long time in coming. Computers were rapidly modernizing every aspect of an industry that had been dependent on archaic technology for generations. I caught on quickly; and when the newsroom retired its old Underwoods and installed computer terminals, the computer company offered me a job. I jumped at it. My brother, who was two and one-half years younger than I, had already married and left for graduate school. So I sold our home, exchanged my Associated Press Style Manual for what felt like one hundred pounds of computer books, and I moved to Boston.

It was a change I anticipated with great joy. The Boston area had a large Jewish population, which I felt dramatically improved my chances of eventually marrying a nice, Jewish man. So, with briefcase in one hand and company Air Travel Card in the other, I said good-bye to Vermont and began flying to newspapers across the country, installing software for computerized phototypesetting systems.

For a small-town girl, it was a dream come true. Although I lived out of a suitcase for months at a time and occasionally longed for a good, home-cooked meal, I loved the work; I loved the travel; I loved my life. Into this idyllic circumstance walked the man I was to marry.

James was unlike anyone I had ever dated. Twenty-five years my senior, he was a successful, high-powered corporate executive who knew what he wanted and was accustomed to getting it. He had a reputation for being smart and self-confident, with a low threshold for incompetence or insubordination. An impeccable dresser, he was extremely handsome, with silver gray hair and clear blue eyes that quickly penetrated even the toughest façade. His quiet, dignified reserve, courtly manners, and charming southern accent, combined with the power he wielded, made him an intimidating presence to many. Yet he treated everyone with equal fairness and respect.

James was a listener, not a talker. He could deftly size up a person after five minutes of conversation. Although he was tenderhearted, considerate, and affectionate, he unmistakably called the shots; he made the decisions, and he comfortably bore the responsibility. In short, he was everything I had ever dreamed of in a husband, with one crucial exception: he wasn't Jewish.

Two people could hardly have been more different. Whereas I was emotional and easily frustrated, James was unflappable. The man never got excited about anything. Even in the most difficult circumstance, he always remained cool, composed, and collected. It was a quality I grew to depend upon.

"How can you stay so calm?" I once asked, agitated to the core about something myself.

"Nothin' to it, honey," he'd say with a smile, a wink, and a snap of his fingers. "When you get excited, you can't think."

The biggest difference, however, was not in our temperaments. It was in our backgrounds. James was a southerner who could trace his lineage all the way back to colonial America, when the king of England is said to have deeded his family a huge tract of property in North Carolina via a land grant. I barely knew my grandparents' names. In his entire life he had never heard a word of Yiddish. He understood nothing of Jewish history, culture, or tradition and knew nothing of the Jewish religion except that it categorically rejected Jesus. He also knew little about the Jewish dietary laws and could not comprehend my horror the first time I looked into his refrigerator and spied a container of what he proudly explained was bacon grease. I almost got sick. Who in the world cooked with that! Chicken fat—now that was a different story.

By the time we met, my parents, of course, had long since passed away. But I didn't have to wonder what they would have thought. Had James been Jewish, they would have been happy. He was a dependable, respected, successful professional who offered me love, security, and material comfort—all the qualities they had prized so highly as essentials for happiness. But he *wasn't* Jewish. He was a *goy* (Gentile); and in the end, that was all that would have mattered. I remembered well how my gentle, devoted father had looked me in the eye and said, "If you ever marry someone who is not Jewish, you'll be dead to me." Dead.

"You'll never be accepted by the *goyim*," he used to tell me. "You're a Jew, and you must stick with your own kind." James came from a big Baptist family that played a vital role in his life. He traveled home to North Carolina every chance he got, and I knew he wanted me to feel that it was home too. I worried for months about how these Gentiles would receive me and how I would feel being around them. Would they accept me, or would I always be "the Jew" who married their brother? These questions did not trouble James in the least. He took enormous pride in his family, particularly in his mother, and assured me they would welcome me and make me feel comfortable.

So in June of 1978 we were married. And that was when I first met Bob.

ENDNOTES

[1] "Country Gazette," Vol. XIII, Issue No. 2, *Country Home,* April 1994, p.101.

[2] Ibid., pp.100-101.

[3] Ibid.

[4] Abba Eban, *Personal Witness, Israel Through My Eyes,* G. P. Putnam's Sons, New York, 1992, p. 69.

[5] Michael Berenbaum, *The World Must Know,* U.S. Holocaust Memorial Museum, Little Brown and Company, Boston, 1993, p.58.

[6] Eban, p.55.

[7] Ibid., p.55.

[8] Ibid., pp.100-102.

[9] Ibid., p.154.

Chapter Two
℗

Thelma

"I don't suppose you'd perform this wedding with a rabbi?" I asked the minister over the telephone, remembering my brother's wedding two years earlier. It took a lot of doing, but my brother had managed to convince a nice, conservative minister (his fiancée was Presbyterian) to share the honors with a rabbi. Finding an amenable rabbi, however, had been more challenging. The man he finally engaged looked like an over-the-hill hippie and had a Star of David made of welded horseshoe nails dangling ponderously from his neck.

His demeanor would never have made it past my father; but my parents were no longer living, and for some reason, my brother didn't care much about the sanctity of the rabbi's credentials. He made certain the minister signed the marriage license.

"No, I wouldn't," came the reply.

"Didn't think so," I said. By now I had resigned myself to the fact that my nuptials were going to be punctuated with the words "Jesus Christ"—words I had used often myself but in an entirely different context.

"I'd like to meet with you and your fiancé first, though," he told me.

Several days later James and I presented ourselves before the pastor of what appeared to be a mammoth Baptist church in Cocoa Beach, Florida, where we had just purchased a house. The church was ideally situated on a throne of expensive beachfront property overlooking the Atlantic Ocean.

This congregation is certainly well-healed, I thought to myself, as we pulled into the parking lot. My innate suspicion of Gentile clergy rose rapidly to the surface. But James had wanted a minister to marry us, and since I doubted that I'd be able to locate both a rabbi and a minister who would be willing to share the honors, I agreed.

As we entered the pastor's study, James immediately extended his hand and introduced us. With a friendly smile, Bob rose from the chair behind his desk to shake hands. I don't know exactly what I had been expecting, but Dr. Robert O. Ferm wasn't it. He was sixty-six at the time, with balding white hair, sympathetic eyes, and a face graced with such a compassionate and friendly smile that he surely had to be someone's much-loved grandfather. His humility found expression in an almost ethereal kindness that I had seen only once before, in the face of the woman who was to become my mother-in-law. First we told him of the difference in our ages, then in our religious backgrounds.

"You know," Bob said pleasantly, looking directly at me, "we have a completed Jew who sings in our choir."

A "completed Jew," I thought. Now there was a moniker for you. What mendacious morsel of Christian terminology was this? Although I had not the foggiest notion what he was talking about, I smiled politely, nodded, and said to myself, "What am I, half a Jew?"

I seemed pretty complete to me, particularly after all those years in Hebrew school. I had studied the Scriptures in Hebrew, had celebrated my bat mitzvah at age thirteen, had attended United Synagogue Youth conventions, had led a Young Judea youth group, had been a counselor at a Jewish camp, and had dated rabbinical students at the Jewish Theological Seminary of America. How much more "complete" did I have to get than that!

"The Old Testament and the New Testament really fit together like a hand in a glove," Bob continued, linking the fingers of both his hands together in front of his chest.

"Well, I don't know," was all I said.

He never pressed the issue. He just smiled warmly then turned to chat with James. James explained that he was divorced and had three grown children. During his first marriage he had ascended to the presidency of almost every do-good organization that had come down the pike, and he had been a regular churchgoer. He had taught Sunday school and had even served on his church's deacon board. Although he believed in attending church, he had fallen away in recent years and feared that his neglectfulness might now impede his entrance through the pearly gates. It appeared that James computed his standing with God to be in direct proportion to his do-gooder involvement. That seemed a reasonable assumption to me. It was, in fact, consistent with Jewish theology, which teaches that Jews must earn their way into God's presence by performing good deeds (mitzvot) and charitable works (tzedakah).

Apparently James and I passed muster because on June 19, Bob and his wife, Dr. Lois Ferm, came to our new home, and in a lovely poolside ceremony, Bob united us as husband and wife. We were only seven in number that day, but it was enough. My brother and his wife were unable to come, but Nancy, my best friend since seventh grade, flew down from Vermont that morning and stood by my side.

I was thrilled to be with Nancy again. Her friendship had seen me through the deaths of my mother, my father, and even my Uncle Saul. In high school and then in college, we shared all the silly things girls share as they grow up, and later we added our heartthrobs and heartaches to those memories.

Like me, Nancy was Jewish. Also like me, she had very much enjoyed talking to the Ferms. Here was a really nice couple, I thought to myself. Both Bob and Lois were warm and friendly, and though it seemed illogical, they appeared to genuinely care about us. Although I had been out on the lawn, I had overheard when the conversation on the patio turned to the subject of Jesus. Nancy told me later that the Ferms had not been pushy or offensive, were respectful of her views, and had been very, very nice. As a matter of fact, an aura of "niceness" seemed to hover about them. Something was different about these people. They were gentle, kind, thoroughly nonjudgmental, and I grew enormously fond of them right away—which was why I agreed to accompany James to church several Sundays later.

"Why do you want to go now?" I asked him. "We've never gone to church before?"

"Well," James replied, "he married us, and I think it would be nice to show up."

So we drove the short distance to the big tabernacle by the sea. When we entered the sanctuary, we immediately realized we were late. The service had started earlier than we had anticipated. As we slid silently into the pew, it suddenly dawned on me that the church was nearly empty. The imposing structure, which had appeared so opulent on the outside, had woefully few congregants on the inside. Fewer than fifty people sat demurely in an auditorium that looked as though it could accommodate the entire National Football League.

We soon learned why. The area had suffered an economic collapse a number of years earlier when the Apollo space program had ended. Many people had moved away in search of work. That fact, coupled with a congregational split, had all but killed the church. Bob had recently been called to pastor in hopes that he could salvage the situation. Thus the proud and stately exterior actually sheltered a very small and humble congregation.

Bob looked up and smiled as we took our seats. I knew none of the hymns, of course, and paid very little attention to what was being said. But out of politeness I nodded and tried to look interested, wondering all the while how much longer until I could go home. Suddenly, three little words captured my attention: *Year of Jubilee.*

How did Dr. Ferm know about that? All at once I was ten years old again, looking out the windows of my Hebrew school.

"Every fifty years," my Hebrew teacher had said, "Israel was to celebrate the Year of Jubilee and proclaim liberty throughout the land." Hebrew slaves were to be set free, and any land that was purchased or otherwise exchanged was to revert back to its original owners. These words had been written by Moses in the Jewish Law—the Torah—the first five books of the Jewish Bible.

How did Bob know what was in the Torah? I began listening. He referred to a number of other Hebrew Scriptures also. It was curious, I thought, that a Gentile would know about these Jewish things. Why would Gentiles bother to concern themselves with the Jewish Law and the Jewish Scriptures? I thought that they were interested only in Jesus and the New Testament. It intrigued me that this man could be right about these Hebrew Scriptures yet be so wrong when it came to Jesus. "Oh well," I thought. "That's *goyim* for you!"

After the service Bob and Lois came over to say hello. They looked so happy to see us and immediately introduced us to several people with whom we shook hands and exchanged pleasantries. Then we left. As we walked to the car, the words *Year of Jubilee* reverberated in my mind, churning up bits of my Hebrew school education that had long lain dormant.

"James," I said, as he put the key in the ignition. "Why don't Jewish people believe in Jesus?"

My husband delayed starting the engine, and we sat there in the church parking lot. Then he turned to look at me and stated plainly, "Honey, I don't know the answer to that. You'll have to ask a rabbi. But I don't believe that Jesus was just a man."

"You don't?" I asked incredulously. "Well, what was he then?"

"I believe he was God come to earth," he replied.

"That's ridiculous," I said. "How could a man be God?"

James didn't hesitate when I scoffed. "Well," he said calmly, "I can believe that God came to earth a lot quicker than I can believe Moses parted the Red Sea."

He turned the key in the ignition and off we drove. But his words had effectively penetrated the outer walls of my theological fortress. I believed unequivocally that God had used Moses to part the Red Sea. I had learned this miracle in Hebrew school. I had *not* been taught some inane little story about Moses knowing where the rocks were, as though the Egyptians were so inept they could not have found them also. Nor was I taught the equal absurdity that the Israelites crossed at low tide or knew a special place where the water was forgiving or crossed not the Red Sea but a little brook that for some inexplicable reason the Egyptians found impossible to ford.

The book of Exodus in the Torah states emphatically that the waters parted and stood like a wall on both sides, with dry land—not mud—forming a path over which the Israelites escaped. That path was wide enough to accommodate a wealth of livestock, untold possessions, and about 2.5 million refugees—a mixed multitude of Israelites and Egyptians that today would equal the entire populations of Vermont, New Hampshire, and Delaware. The Egyptians tried to pursue; but when they reached the midst of the sea, the waters returned to their former place and covered them completely.

I had been a newspaper reporter. I was accustomed to dealing with fact, not fiction. It didn't take a brick to fall on my head for me to realize that whatever happened at the Red Sea involved no trifling amount of water. It was substantial enough to drown an entire Egyptian army—horses, chariots, and all. That miracle was part of my Jewish heritage. It was what I was taught. It was the only explanation for the Exodus that made logical sense, and it was what I believed.

Either God existed or He didn't. And if He existed, which I believed, then He was *all* mighty and *all* knowing or He would not be God. Therefore, as God Almighty, He could do whatever He chose. Parting the waters to let the Jewish people escape over dry land did not exactly strain Him. Thus, if He could send plagues and famines; if He could smite the first-born of all Egyptian males, whether beast or man; if He could provide manna from heaven and bring the Israelites into the land of Canaan against all odds, then He could do anything.

I sat in the car quietly as we drove away. As a reporter, I had made my living by searching for the truth. Now, when it came to a subject as important as God, I wasn't sure what was true anymore. Questions came tumbling into my mind.

What if God really *had* decided to come to earth? Since He was all powerful, who could stop Him? Hadn't He said through the prophet Isaiah, "Yea, before the day was, I am he; and there is none that can deliver out of my hand; I will work, and who shall hinder it?" (Isa. 43:13). In other words, God could do whatever He wished whenever He wished or He wouldn't be God. What if He had come in the person of Jesus? Who in the world *was* Jesus, anyway?

Then, as I was riding in the car, a terrifying thought suddenly gripped me. What if the Jewish people were wrong? What if we have been wrong for almost two thousand years? What if I did not really know the truth?

James, preoccupied with driving and unaware of my thoughts, asked where I wanted to go for lunch. We chatted, decided on a nice restaurant, and soon the conversation put the subject out of mind.

I spent the next few months concentrating on being married. I took my first stab at decorating a new home, learning how to cook (an uphill battle if ever there was one), adjusting to Florida, and becoming a good wife.

But unbeknown to me, a seed had been planted—a tiny little speck that began to germinate quietly in the recesses of my mind. Every so often, without warning, I would find myself wondering *what if*. I did not know it, but the search had begun.

"Now, you carry this," Thelma Bennett said to my sister-in-law, carefully placing containers heaped with home-cooked delicacies into a box to be delivered to an ailing woman down the road. "And James," she said, turning to her eldest son, "you carry this."

James's box, destined for a different unfortunate soul, was equally well stocked with ham, turkey, the traditional oyster dressing, sweet potato pudding, rice, butter beans (no authentic southern meal, I was discovering, was complete without them), biscuits so tender they melted in your mouth, and several slices of the finest pecan pie I had ever tasted.

It was my first Christmas at the family homestead, and food was going out the door as fast as people were coming in. The house was overflowing with as many members of the considerably sized clan as could make it home for the holidays. The telephone rang mercilessly for my mother-in-law who, I had concluded, was the most popular woman in the county.

Thelma was in her mid-70s by the time I had entered the family. She lived alone on the farm in North Carolina where she had reared all seven of her children. But how she actually found time to be alone was beyond me. If the doorbell wasn't ringing, the telephone was. She had a handle on everything going on for miles around, and despite her sweet countenance and soft voice, she was—make no mistake—very much in charge.

"Mama," protested one of my sisters-in-law, "I don't understand why you want to give her anything. She was never very nice to you."

"The Bible says we're not to repay evil with evil," Mrs. Bennett replied, cramming the box so full of food it looked ready to split in two. The intended recipient of the feast was an aged woman who had been forsaken by her children and whose debilitating maladies compounded her misery. She was going to get this food, and that was that.

James shook his head and chuckled. He was proud of his mother's generosity and knew it was no use arguing with her anyway. "Come on," he said with a smile as he beckoned to his sister. "Let's go." They loaded the boxes into the car and off they drove down the country road.

It seemed as though parts of every meal we ate except for breakfast made it into containers of some sort that my mother-in-law insisted be "carried," as she put it, to someone or other. She was the most giving person I had ever seen. Nothing new stayed around long enough to get old because it always wound up being given to someone else. One year for Mother's Day I sent her flowers, which she later confessed ended up at the hospital bedside of one of her friends.

"I enjoyed them, and I thought she would enjoy them too. I knew you'd understand," she told me. I did. I understood that one of her greatest pleasures in life was helping others.

But there was much about her I did not understand. She had little use for the material goods of this world—unless, of course, she could give them away. She wanted her home neat and clean, with her appliances operating on all thrusters. But beyond that, she was content with vintage furniture, familiar knick-knacks, and linoleum floors in all her rooms, including the living room.

Her children were all well off and more than willing to give her anything she wanted. She just didn't want much. Over the years they had managed to install central air-conditioning, security lighting, an emergency medical system, and several other conveniences that she allowed. But she refused to let them do all that they wanted, which included installing a dishwasher and wall-to-wall carpeting, among other things. "I have no use for finery," she once told me.

She had no use for many other things too. She did not tolerate smoking, drinking, or cursing. Her stand on these vices was so well known in the community that any drunkard or cusser who entered her home left both liquor and language on the other side of the threshold.

A petite woman with hair as white as snow and James's clear blue eyes, Thelma had an irresistible smile, a quick wit, and a sense of hearing so keen she knew from the back bedroom what you were saying in the kitchen. She was compassionate, tenderhearted, and empathized deeply with other people, whose troubles she seemed to know intimately.

We would talk for hours, usually while she was cooking. Mrs. Bennett was born in North Carolina, not far from where she was then living. She never really knew her father, who died when she was a just a child. Later her mother remarried and gave Thelma a half-sister to whom she was devoted all her life. Then her mother died, her stepfather remarried and had more children, and my mother-in-law became a type of Cinderella. She worked hard, scrubbing, cooking, and cleaning. According to one of the older men in the community, Thelma had been a beauty, more beautiful even than her five daughters had been—and according to my husband, that was saying something. She had had suitors aplenty, but she told me the only one who ever captured her heart was Barney Bennett. She married him when she was eighteen and brought her half-sister, then in seventh grade, to live with them, rearing her as one of her own children.

I never knew my father-in-law. James spoke of him frequently in tones of unmitigated adoration. He had died of a massive stroke more than twenty-five years earlier, at only fifty-two. He was sitting in a chair one evening calculating the price of a crop when, without warning, he slumped over dead. Thelma suddenly was left with a farm she had no idea how to run and the two youngest of her seven children still in high school.

"I didn't know what to do," Mrs. Bennett told me during one of our lengthy talks in the kitchen as she sat with a dishpan in her lap, snapping green beans that she had just picked from her garden. "But I knew the Lord would help me." She talked about "the Lord" all the time. It was as though He were an ordinary member of the family. He was her helper, companion, provider, and counselor all rolled into one. She consulted Him about everything, and He always seemed to assist her.

One time, she told me, her husband had been bitten by a rattlesnake. Somehow my father-in-law had managed to get himself and his youngest son, who was with him, safely home before collapsing into a coma. Since he was extremely prominent in the county, news traveled fast that Mr. Bennett lay dying. Soon the farmhouse was teeming with people. Thelma, given to hospitality, immediately gathered what food she could to provide for her guests.

"I had only one loaf of bread," she said. "So many people were coming in and out I didn't know what to do. I just prayed to the Lord and asked Him to make sure I had enough. And you know," she said, her blue eyes misting with tears, "everyone had sandwiches, and there was bread left over. I do believe the Lord blessed that loaf of bread just like He blessed the loaves and the fishes."

It didn't matter that I knew nothing about loaves and fishes. She did. She believed that the Lord had multiplied her bread just as she believed the New Testament account of Jesus having turned five loaves and two small fish into enough food to satisfy thousands of hungry people. She also believed that the Lord had answered her prayers in restoring Barney's health after that harrowing experience.

Yes, God had answered her prayers—something He apparently did on a regular basis. Her relationship with Him was conspicuously personal. Thelma had no formal religious training. She never went to college, never had a career, and seldom ventured more than a few hours' drive from home. Most of her life had been devoted to church work, caring for her family, and providing a good home-cooked meal for anyone in the community who needed one. Her closets were bursting with quilts that she had painstakingly pieced together over the years from scraps of old clothes, which were also the result of her handiwork.

When he was a boy, James said, the only items he ever knew his mother to purchase were sugar and flour. Everything else she made herself.

"Even butter?" I asked.

"Even butter."

"What about ketchup? She couldn't possibly have made ketchup!" I said, protesting.

"She made her own ketchup," he told me.

Her thriftiness, good sense in managing her household, and her tireless hard work reminded me of my own mother. But there was one colossal difference. For her, when you were dead, you still weren't dead.

Mrs. Bennett functioned on the uncomplicated premise that every word in her Bible was a word from the mouth of God. And she fervently believed that the same God who had divided the Red Sea for Moses was the same God who loved her, who took care of her, who answered her prayers, who had multiplied her bread, and who would eventually carry her to heaven. Of that she had no doubt.

She had peace. She had hope. She had joy. She had all the things that money could not buy; and it was becoming abundantly clear to me that they were all the result of her faith in Jesus. She believed that this Jesus of hers was the second person in a unified, three-part Godhead, thus making Him fully God. As such, He had forgiven her sins and had prepared a home for her in heaven that no one could ever take away. It was space reserved in her name, and she was as certain of it as though she had already been there. I would have given anything if my mother had had the same assurance.

Life after death is not a subject most Jewish people think about. When it came up in Hebrew school, it was usually disposed of in one tidy sentence: "The body returns to the ground, and the soul returns to the Lord."

Every soul? The likelihood of *every* soul returning to the Lord was simply not logical. What about the wicked? Surely Moses, Abraham, and Adolph Hitler were not going to be roomies in heaven. Where was justice then? A just and righteous God would surely reserve a place of suffering for evil men. Even King David of Israel confirmed that fact in Psalm 9 when he said, "The wicked shall be turned into hell, and all the nations that forget

God" (Ps. 9:17 KJV). Yet David would "dwell in the house of the LORD forever" (Ps. 23:6).

No, it was not the existence of heaven and hell that began troubling me. According to the Hebrew Scriptures, they unquestionably existed. What I was becoming increasingly concerned with, however, was how a person could ensure entrance into the former rather than the latter. Even though I was still in my late twenties, I had no delusions concerning my mortality. I had covered enough fatalities as a reporter, had seen enough body bags, and had buried enough loved ones to know I was not going to live forever. Someday I would die. Perhaps I would die young. Perhaps not. But now I was beginning to worry about where I would go when that event occurred.

In Hebrew school we all assumed that decent people went to heaven. You did unto others as you would have them do unto you, and you tried to be a good person. Of course, defining "good" was a little tricky.

You certainly could not measure "good" by obedience to Jewish Law, because the Law was so extensive and cumbersome that nobody could fully keep it. Besides, even within Judaism, the rabbis disagreed fiercely. So "good" depended, for the most part, upon whose yardstick you were using. Most people I knew just deferred to whatever yardstick suited them best based on societal norms of the day and the social circles in which they traveled.

In that context, I didn't think I faired too badly. Although I had done plenty of things I was not proud of— and others I was downright ashamed of—I managed to push those weights aside because of all the people I knew who had done as I had. Besides, I reasoned, what was past, was past. On the other hand, I never smoked; I rarely drank; I never did drugs; I had even quit swearing.

Would I go to heaven? I had no idea. I always thought I would, but as I plowed through my memory, digging up one Jewish teaching after another, I overturned nothing that gave me assurance that when I died I would be with God. Nor did I turn up any modern-day procedure that I could follow that would guarantee me forgiveness for the transgressions I had already committed.

Had I lived in the days of the kings of Judah, I would have known what to do. I could have followed the Torah and brought a sacrifice, usually a lamb without spot or blemish, to the Temple in Jerusalem. There I would have laid my hand on the animal's head, symbolically transferring my sin to the head of the innocent sacrifice. The animal would have been killed in my place, and the blood would have been placed on the altar to make atonement for my sin, in accordance with the commands God gave Moses for the Jewish people:

> For the life of the flesh is in the blood; and I have given it to you upon the altar to make an atonement for your souls; for it is the blood that maketh an atonement for the soul (Lev. 17:11).

But I had no Temple. For some inexplicable reason, the same God who had commanded that forgiveness of sin be sought through blood sacrifice had allowed the total destruction of the only place on earth where He had commanded that sacrifice to be made. In A.D. 70 the Romans sacked Jerusalem and burned the second—and last—Temple to the ground. All that remains today that is of consequence to the Jewish people is the retaining wall on the western side of the Temple Mount. It is often referred to as the Wailing Wall.

Without the ability to offer a sacrifice, how then could I follow God's instructions for obtaining forgiveness? I could not. No one could. From my earliest days, I remember sitting in Hebrew school wondering why God would do that to His people? Why would He command us to do something that He knew, down the road, we would never be able to do? Why would He leave us without a way to obtain forgiveness for our sins?

I suppose the rabbis asked themselves the same question, because after the Temple was destroyed, they established another system entirely. That was the system that I looked to, the one that told me entrance into heaven was based on the preponderance of my good deeds. I was taught that God somehow weighed your good deeds against your bad, and if He was pleased, you were in. Obtaining the acceptable degree of goodness, however, did not appear an exacting science.

How many good deeds would make me good enough to go to heaven? How many good deeds would it take to counterbalance a bad one? Could several really bad deeds eradicate my good deeds? How could I find out how I was doing? What precisely must I do to improve my standing? What if I've done the best I can, but God doesn't think it's good enough? Where will I end up when I die? The celestial scale theory was nebulous at best. Not only did it provide no guarantees, it relegated you to a lifetime of uncertainty concerning your eternal destination.

Judaism, of course, is not the only religion that revolves around human effort. So does Catholicism, for example. Some of these questions had come up once before when I worked as a reporter. A group of us had gone out to eat and were pontificating on different aspects of religion. A colleague of mine who was particularly adept in the art of asking questions told us that he had grown up in the Roman Catholic Church, which distinguishes between venial (minor) sins and mortal sins. A person can be cleansed of venial sins by serving time in purgatory, he said, then scoot on through the pearly gates. But mortal sin results in everlasting torment in the life beyond.

One day, he said, attendance at youth group had waned beyond acceptable limits. The students were promptly informed that skipping youth group had been upgraded to a mortal sin.

"Well," said my friend, "that didn't sound right, so I began questioning my priest. First I asked him how you know when you've jumped from committing venial sins to mortal sins. So I asked him what kind of sin it would be if I stole money from a poor man.

"'That would be a mortal sin,' my priest said. Then I asked him what kind of sin it would be if I stole money from a rich man. 'That would be a venial sin,' my priest said. Then I asked him what kind of sin it would be if I stole a little money from a poor man. 'That would be a venial sin,' my priest said. 'What about a lot of money from a rich man?'

"'That would be a mortal sin,' he said. After a few more go-arounds like that," my friend said with a laugh, "I finally concluded that the difference between a venial sin and a mortal sin was $37.50!"

We all had a good chuckle and dismissed the entire subject as an exercise in futility. Unless you could ask God Himself how you were doing, there apparently was no way to know. Certainly the Holy One of Israel must have a better system than that well-meaning priest had. But what was it?

I never asked Mrs. Bennett, and she never volunteered the information. She did, however, tell me that she "got converted" when she was fifteen. *Conversion* was certainly a term I had heard before. To my people, it embodied about fifteen hundred years' worth of Christendom's nefarious attempts to rid the world of Jews. Throughout history we were threatened to either convert or die. As early as the fifth and sixth centuries in the Roman Empire, attacks began on synagogues, and anti-Jewish legislation reared its hateful head. In the old Visigothic Kingdom, later known as Spain, Jews were ordered to convert to Catholicism or get out. Many fled. Others converted but secretly practiced Judaism. Then things got worse. Around A.D. 700 anyone caught being a secret Jew was sold into slavery, and persons even suspected of being Jewish lost their children, who were given to Gentile clergy to be reared.[1]

Similar events followed the children of Israel everywhere they went. Perhaps one of the best known was the Spanish Inquisition. Until the end of the fourteenth century, Jewish communities had actually flourished in Spain. The Jews, many of them highly educated, had served the Catholic monarchs faithfully, helped the economy with their commerce, and held high and trusted positions in government.[2]

Their success, however, fomented jealousy. In 1391 a monk by the name of Ferrand Martinez incited such vicious anti-Semitism that Catholic mobs tore through Seville, Cordova, Toledo, and other cities and all but annihilated the large Jewish communities there. The movement spread like wildfire. Throughout the fifteenth century in Spain, Jewish people were threatened to accept the cross or die. Tens of thousands converted.

Rather than being accepted by the Catholics, however, these *conversos* were hated. It wasn't enough that they had been forced to forsake Judaism at the point of a sword. Now they were being called *Marranos*, which meant "pigs."[3] Bloody riots broke out, and the Catholics did everything in their power to pressure the Spanish throne into discriminating against the *conversos*.

In response to this outcry, the Inquisition came to Spain in 1480. Its chief mission was to seek out half-hearted Jewish converts and torture them into either submission or death. The Inquisition had long been an arm of the Roman Catholic Church, but most monarchs hesitated to ask Rome to establish it in their kingdoms because it became a beast that devoured everything within its reach. Its power was immense. It functioned independently of a country's legal system, its proceedings were secret, and it devoted itself entirely to prying into people's private lives in an effort to ferret out and punish anyone who deviated from Catholic doctrine.[4] Its inquisitors were ruthless men who used utterly diabolical tortures to extract confessions.

Between 1478 and 1808, when the Inquisition officially ended, 323,362 people had been burned.[5] The vast majority of these were Jewish men, women, and children who were set on fire in the town square amid great festivity and chants praising God. All were converts to Catholicism. The converted Jews who, after torture, repented of having secretly practiced Judaism and confessed the Roman Catholic Church to be the sole source of salvation, were graciously strangled before they were burned.[6]

The Inquisition, however, had no power over unconverted Jews. To remedy that vexation, Grand Inquisitor Tomás de Torquemada persuaded the Catholic kings and Queen Isabella to purify the nation and the faith by immediately expelling from Spain all Jews who refused to be baptized. The expulsion of the Jews finalized the tragic dismemberment of the largest Jewish community in the world at that time.

On August 2, 1492, not knowing where they would end up or if they would even live to tell the tale, the final remains of the Jewish community departed Spanish soil by boat. The same day, three little vessels, the Nina, the Pinta, and the Santa Maria, departed from the harbor near Seville, sailing directly past the ships carrying the Jewish exiles. Christopher Columbus noted the fact in his diary.[7]

I knew the word *conversion*, all right; and I was not about to let it happen to me. I was born a Jew and I would die a Jew. But it puzzled me that Mrs. Bennett claimed to have been converted. What on earth did she get converted *to*? She was born a Baptist and was still a Baptist. How did that constitute *conversion*? I pondered the question for a while, then let it slide. I never interrogated her concerning religion. Instead, I watched her like a hawk.

By 5:30 every morning she was already in the kitchen, reading her Bible and praying. That Bible was so worn out she must have read it a million times, but still she kept on reading it. I had read a substantial amount of the Jewish Bible in Hebrew school, but most of the time I had found it irrelevant and difficult to understand. So what was my mother-in-law reading that held her attention so raptly?

After reading, she would pray. She simply bowed her head and talked to the Lord as though He were a close and respected friend who had sat down beside her and had asked how things were going. It didn't really matter to me that Thelma prayed to Jesus. As far as I was concerned, there was only one Lord capable of listening—my Lord— the God of Abraham, Isaac, and Jacob. And for some reason, He was definitely listening to her.

She poured her heart out to him, praying for people by name and asking Him to heal this one, strengthen that one, provide money to pay bills for yet another, so on and so forth. When she knew someone's need, she prayed about it. When she did not know specifics, she prayed generally, asking the Lord to provide as He saw fit, always thanking Him for the prayers He had already answered and for the works He had already accomplished.

I marveled at how personal her prayers were and how easily she petitioned the great God of the universe to stretch forth His hand into the trivial, insignificant matters of everyday life. And for her, He stretched forth His hand on a regular basis.

Thelma loved to retell the stories of answered prayer. With tears in her eyes, she once told me the account of a little girl who had come from an exceedingly poor family. The child desperately wanted nothing more for Christmas than a pair of new, red shoes. The family could barely afford food. Shoes were out of the question.

Not wanting her child to be overcome with grief on Christmas morning, the mother had tried to dissuade her daughter from believing that God would answer such a prayer. But the girl was not to be dissuaded. Sometime before church on Christmas day, there came a knock at the door. A neighbor, completely unaware of the child's desire, had brought a package.

"I have no use for these," she said, "and I was wondering if anyone here could use them." Inside the box was a beautiful pair of brand new, red shoes, exactly the right size for the trusting little girl.

In all my life I had never been taught to pray as that little girl had—simply and sincerely, believing He would attend to the everyday cares of my life. I did sometimes talk to God in my own words, but it was not often. Such prayer is not standard fare in Judaism. All our prayers are liturgical. They come from a Hebrew prayer book called a *Sidur*. There are prayers to recite in the morning, prayers to recite in the evening, prayers to recite when someone dies, prayers to recite on the Sabbath, prayers for lighting candles, etc. I can still recite some of them in Hebrew today.

While growing up, I had attended synagogue every Sabbath and had participated in the junior congregation service—an abbreviated, hour-long service conducted entirely by the youth. When I celebrated my bat mitzvah at age thirteen, I sang a three-page *Haftorah* (portion of Scripture other than Torah) and subsequently ended up in the adult choir, which sang at Friday night services.

"You're so Jewish you should be a rabbi," my friend Nancy once told me. Nancy had perceived the substance of my identity. I enjoyed being Jewish. My life found security in the richness of Jewish culture and tradition, and my theology hung comfortably on the Hebrew school teaching I had been privileged to enjoy.

How, then, could Thelma, a Baptist and a follower of Jesus, enjoy such a close personal relationship with God? She had a pipeline to the Almighty, all right. It was as plain as day to see. But that was not what I envied; it was the Almighty's pipeline to her. He seemed to communicate with her. No matter how rough the waters became, she knew He loved her and she loved Him. They enjoyed an intimacy with each other that brought her peace in the midst of turmoil, joy in the midst of heartache, and absolute assurance that He would one day usher her into His divine presence for all eternity.

She did not see God as an awesome judge, weighing her good deeds against her bad. She believed that her bad had been unconditionally forgiven. She already knew her eternal destination—and it was heaven. She had her ticket in her hand, stamped and ready to go.

I had never seen such a thing before, and I wanted it. I had everything I had ever thought would make me happy. I had married for love, and fortunately for me, my husband also provided stability and financial security. I had a good marriage, a good profession, a nice home, and material prosperity. But it all paled in comparison to what Thelma had. I had an emptiness where her cup was running over. And what made things worse was that I knew her cup was somehow being filled through faith in Jesus, and Jesus was not for Jews.

ENDNOTES

[1] Solomon Grayzel, *A History of the Jews*, The Jewish Publication Society of America, Philadelphia; 2nd Edition, 3rd Impression, 1977, p. 303.

[2] "Spain," *Encyclopaedia Britannica*, 1972, Vol. 20, p. 1092.

[3] Grayzel, p. 408.

[4] Grayzel, p. 409.

[5] Jason L. Slade, *The Spanish Inquisition*, [http://www.iem.rwth-aachen.de/~groening/spanish.html] August 6, 1996, p. 4.

[6] Grayzel, p. 411.

[7] Grayzel, p. 415.

Chapter Three

☙

Paid in Full

"Lorna!"

Immediately I knew something was wrong. Barely awake and still in my nightgown, I rushed into the kitchen at the sound of my husband's voice. There stood James, unable to move and slumped over the countertop, which he was clutching with both hands in an attempt to keep himself from collapsing on the floor.

"Oh, no," I thought, trying to keep from panicking. "He's had another heart attack!"

James had survived a major heart attack a number of years before I had met him. Yet he had told me many times that he had made such a complete recovery he had been pronounced the picture of health by his doctor, who was satisfied with regulating only his blood pressure. Although my husband's job frequently took him on trips across the country, in the nine months we had been married he still managed to indulge his passion for golf almost every week-end and got adequate rest. How could this have happened?

"What's wrong?" I asked frantically, removing his jacket and tie. It was obvious that five minutes more and he would have been out the door and in the car en route to work. My greatest fear was that he would have a heart attack while he was driving, and he would die alone in a ditch, pinned under the wreckage of his automobile.

I put his right arm over my shoulder and with my left arm, grabbed hold of him around his waist, trying to support his weight until we made it to the bedroom where he could lie down.

"My leg," was all he could say. The pain was so great he could hardly speak. James was not a complainer, and I had learned by now that his strong will and devotion to self-discipline allowed him to suffer intense pain in silence.

"It's my leg," he said again. "I wish they would cut it off."

His left leg had bothered him recently. Attributing the problem to muscle cramps, his doctor had prescribed muscle relaxants that my husband took faithfully.

"I was reaching in the cupboard to get a glass for orange juice when it happened," he said.

I immediately got through to his doctor and related the facts.

"It's his back," came the response. "It's his back. It's been his back all along," he said, realizing now that he had misdiagnosed his patient. "Get an ambulance and get him to the hospital."

I pulled on some jeans and the maternity top I had recently finished sewing on my mother's little black Featherweight, just in time to meet the ambulance workers at the door. They lifted my husband onto a stretcher, carried him into the ambulance, closed the door, and took off.

Under different circumstances, the hour-long drive down the coast to the hospital in Melbourne would have been a welcome treat. But not today. Not even the dazzling Florida sunshine could dispel the gloom I felt as I trailed the ambulance in my car, wondering all the while what was wrong with my husband. Almost as soon as we arrived, James was wheeled directly into a private room. No one knew exactly what was causing his problem, but everyone agreed that it emanated from the general area of his back. Soon the doctors started arriving. His doctor came first, followed by the specialists—one after another. They performed several elementary tests in my presence while James lay in bed, then discussed his situation in terminology I could not understand.

The next day was devoted to x-rays. Since I was four months pregnant, I was not allowed in the area and waited by myself until the orderlies wheeled my husband back to me. Nothing showed. His pain had not subsided despite medication. The following day brought still more tests and more inconclusive results. Then a surgeon showed up, scratched the bottom of his foot, and immediately pronounced that he had some type of tumor—possibly on his spine—which would require surgery.

Tumor. That was one piece of medical jargon I understood well. They came in two varieties: malignant and benign. In that one horrific moment, I realized that I might be sentenced to watch my husband die inch by inch from cancer as I had watched my mother. The thought of losing James frightened me. I was profoundly in love with him, and in many respects, I felt that he was all I had in the world. My brother and his wife lived up north, and despite our best efforts, we had drifted apart. I was twenty-eight when James and I married. I had waited for the right man, and now I could not imagine life without him.

"How can you be sure he has a tumor?" I asked the doctor.

"The signs indicate that that's what he has," said the surgeon who had scratched the bottom of his foot.

"You mean to tell me that the little test you just did leads you to conclude that the pain in his leg is coming from a tumor?"

"That's right."

"So what's the next step?" I asked. "What are you going to do? Are you going to operate?"

"We're scheduling him for surgery the day after tomorrow. Meanwhile, we'll take some more x-rays and run some more tests."

James was lying on the bed not saying a word. I knew he was scared. He had never had surgery of any kind. Although I did not want to say anything for fear of upsetting him, I was terrified too. Watching my mother suffer with one operation after another had sufficiently drained me of any hope regarding the success of surgically removing cancer.

I could not believe this was happening. My idyllic little life was suddenly ripping apart. While James rested, I went downstairs to the lobby to call Nancy, who by now had moved from Vermont to California. Standing in the phone booth, I managed, between sobs, to tell her what was happening. I explained, as best I could, the brain scan scheduled for that afternoon.

"They're looking for a tumor," I told her. "What if he has cancer? I just can't face this. Not after my mother." Nancy tried to comfort me, but she knew all too well what my mother had endured, and she was the only other person on earth who truly understood how much James meant to me.

I drove home that night to the loneliness of a dark, quiet house. With nothing to do but think, I conjured up every worst-case scenario. What if James died? What if he became crippled? And on and on and on. There I was, nine months married, four months pregnant, no parents, a brother who lived a thousand miles away, a best friend who lived on the other side of the country, and a husband who might be dying of cancer. I had seen the limitations of modern medicine and placed scant faith in it. If God cared about me, now would be a good time for Him to show it.

I was never taught that God loved me. Nothing in all my Jewish experience had brought God into that personal a realm. He cared for mankind, yes. He cared for the Jewish people, yes. But me? Lorna? Where was it written that the sovereign God of all the universe cared for *me*?

Why, then, was my mother-in-law so sure that He cared for *her*? What source was she tapping into that gave her such unshakable certainty in the love of God? Who was this Jesus of hers? What was she getting from her faith that I was not able to get from mine?

I thought about the conversation James and I had had in the car driving home from church not long after we were married. "I believe Jesus was God come to earth," he had said.

What if James and his mother were right? What if Jesus actually was God? What if God *had* come to earth? He had, in truth, done that very thing in the first book of the Bible, Genesis. But He had paid only a brief visit. In Genesis 18, the Hebrew Scriptures teach that God came to Abraham in the heat of the day, ate a non-kosher meal with him, and promised that Abraham's wife, Sarah, would give birth to a son the following year. The Lord even permitted Abraham to haggle with Him over the number of righteous souls it would take to avert the destruction of Sodom and Gomorrah.

What if the God of Israel had come again, but this time in the person of Jesus? What if God had actually *decided* to be born of a woman, odd as that may seem? Who could stop Him? But why would He do such a thing? Just a short time earlier, I had heard a Jewish man on television claim that Jesus was the Messiah of Israel. Suddenly I was over- whelmed with a horrifying thought. What if my people had failed to recognize the coming of the Messiah? That unwelcome prospect opened the door to questions I did not even want to consider.

Yet, as a reporter, I had been taught to pry open every can and turn over every rock in search of truth. What was the truth about Jesus? Had Judaism somehow fallen victim to error that I had unquestioningly accepted as truth? How could I find out? I refused to consult a rabbi because, in all likelihood, he knew no more about Jesus than I did and would do everything he could to prevent me from defect- ing to Christianity. And I certainly couldn't trust a minis- ter, who I felt sure would try to convert me.

So I began with what was already in my head—my Jewish education. If there was one consistent thread that ran through all my years of Hebrew school, it was the faithless- ness and disobedience of my people. From the time we fled Egypt around 1446 B.C. to the time we became captives in Babylon, some 860 years later, we constantly provoked God. Our whining and complaining persisted even after the Lord had miraculously divided the Red Sea; and it grew so intense that Moses finally cried out, "What shall I do unto this people? They are almost ready to stone me" (Ex. 17:4).

While waiting for Moses to descend from Mount Sinai with the Ten Commandments, the Israelites so provoked the Lord by worshiping a golden calf that God declared to Moses,

I have seen this people, and, behold, it is a stiff-necked people. Now therefore let me alone, that my wrath may burn against them, and that I may consume them: and I will make of thee a great nation (Ex. 32:9–10).

Only Moses' intercessory prayer saved them. Then came the Kadesh Barnea fiasco. Moses sent twelve men (one established leader from each of the twelve tribes) to do reconnaissance work. They were to spy out the Promised Land and report back. Instead of encouraging the Israelites to trust in their great God to bring them into a good land flowing with milk and honey, the report bemoaned the strength of the Canaanites and all but convinced everyone to return to Egypt (Num. 14:3-4).

Only Caleb (the spy from the tribe of Judah) and Joshua (the spy from Ephraim) evidenced faith. They passionately disagreed with the evil report of the other ten, tore their clothes as a sign of mourning, and pleaded with the Israelites to trust the Lord. The result? "But all the congregation demanded to stone them with stones" (Num. 14:10). Not surprisingly, God had had it.

How long will this people provoke me? And how long will it be before they believe me, for all the signs which I have shown among them? . . . How long shall I bear with this evil congregation, who murmur against me? I have heard the murmurings of the children of Israel, which they murmur against me (Num. 14:11, 27).

God was ready to destroy them. Again Moses intervened. But this time the Israelites' unbelief cost them dearly. The Lord sentenced the descendants of Abraham to wander in the desert for forty years, one year for each day the spies were in the land of Canaan. With the exception of Joshua and Caleb, whose faith God rewarded, the Lord condemned everyone twenty years and older to die in the wilderness. And die there they did. Except for Joshua and Caleb, not a single soul who came out of Egypt at age twenty or older ever entered the Promised Land.

The newly formed nation was not off to an auspicious start. Yet things did not improve much as the centuries went by. Over and over, for hundreds of years, prophet after prophet begged, pleaded, and warned the children of Israel to repent and turn to the Lord in faith. The result was always the same. My people stoned, beat, ridiculed, humiliated, rejected, and ultimately ignored the men whom God sent to them.

God constantly railed at the nation, promising judgment if it did not repent. But His warnings did no good. Through Isaiah, the Lord declared,

> *Hear, O heavens, and give ear, O earth; for the LORD hath spoken: I have nourished and brought up children, and they have rebelled against me. The ox knoweth his owner, and the ass, his master's crib, but Israel doth not know; my people doth not consider.*

> *Ah, sinful nation, a people laden with iniquity, a seed of evildoers, children that are corrupters; they have forsaken the LORD, they have provoked the Holy One of Israel unto anger, they are gone away backward* (Isa. 1:2-4).

Isaiah lived to see God mete out the punishment He promised to the northern ten tribes of Israel. They were swept into captivity at the brutal hands of Assyria. By the time Jeremiah arrived on the scene (approximately fifty years after Isaiah had departed from it), all that remained in Jewish control was the southern kingdom of Judah—and it was well on its way to judgment too. Yet the Judeans still failed to get the message that God was serious about punishing their sin.

God was particularly disgusted with the leadership. Calling them corrupt and self-serving, He blamed the Jewish leaders for teaching the people error and causing them to sin: "For the leaders of this people cause them to err; and they who are led of them are destroyed" (Isa. 9:16). "My people have been lost sheep; their shepherds have caused them to go astray" (Jer. 50:6).

These corrupt "shepherds" only confirmed the truth of God's Word by tormenting the messengers who proclaimed it. Jeremiah, for example, was thrown down a well, where he would have died had not one of the king's eunuchs saved him. His family mocked him. The king of Judah burned the manuscripts on which he had recorded the words of God. The Jewish leaders called him a traitor because he told them to submit to God's judgment at the hand of the Babylonians; and after Jerusalem fell in 586 B.C., Jeremiah's Jewish enemies kidnapped him and carted him to Egypt where he died.

Even the seventy-year-long Babylonian Captivity did not melt the hearts of the Israelites. God placed Ezekiel the prophet among the exiles so the people would not be left without a word from the Lord. "But," God counseled Ezekiel, "the house of Israel will not harken unto thee; for they will not hearken unto me; for all the house of Israel are impudent and hard-hearted" (Ezek. 3:7). In the second chapter of Ezekiel, God denounces the nation as "rebellious" in almost every verse.

You would think that after losing their land, losing their sovereignty, and tasting such formidable punishment, the Israelites would change. For a while, the prospects seemed good. When they returned from captivity and rebuilt the Temple, they finally seemed to be turning their hearts toward God and sincerely attempting to heed the greatest commandment in the Jewish Scriptures: "And thou shalt love the LORD thy God with all thine heart, and with all thy soul, and with all thy might" (Dt. 6:5).

Yet about one hundred years after they began returning to their land, my ancestors were right back where they started. The priests were corrupt, the teachers taught error, the people disobeyed the Lord, and all had hearts that were far from God. They even abused the sacrificial system. Instead of bringing the pick of their flocks to the altar as commanded, they brought the blind, the lame, the sick, and the worthless. God was livid.

> Should I accept this of your hand? saith the LORD. . . . for I am a great King (Mal. 1:13–14).

> I have no pleasure in you, saith the LORD of hosts, neither will I accept an offering at your hand. . . . for my name shall be great among the nations, saith the LORD of hosts. But ye have profaned it (Mal. 1:10–12).

As the facts poured in, a distressing pattern emerged. An honest, objective look at the nation of Israel through the eyes of the Hebrew Scriptures was not exactly a comforting sight. I had come from a nation whose own Bible conscientiously traced its rebelliousness and sinfulness. We even lost our land due to disobedience and never really got it back until 1948—and then only a portion of it amid never-ending strife. Sooner or later I had to face the fact that when it came to discerning the things of God, my people had a downright dismal track record.

Something was wrong here. All my life I had accepted the rabbinical interpretation of Judaism as absolute truth simply because I was a Jew. I never questioned the source nor examined the evidence, as I had with most other things. But if I were sick and needing medical care, how likely would I be to go to a doctor who routinely misdiagnosed his patients, botched his operations, and prescribed bad medicine? Yet I was literally staking my soul not on what the Scriptures themselves said but on what the rabbis—the modern-day shepherds—said.

And what they said did not agree with the Bible. Moses, for example, said I needed a blood sacrifice to obtain forgiveness of sin. But the shepherds said I did not. God's prophet Isaiah said "all our righteousnesses [good deeds] are as filthy rags" (Isa. 64:6). But the rabbis said my good deeds could make me good enough to go to heaven. Something here just did not add up; and if my "shepherds" were wrong yet again, where did that leave me?

The next day James underwent tests to locate the elusive tumor. This time he had a myelogram. He was injected with dye, and pictures were taken of his spine. To prevent the dye from traveling throughout his body, he was required to lie perfectly still for twenty-four hours afterward. For me, those twenty-four hours held nothing but agonizing uncertainty. Many times I just wanted to cry but forced myself to remain calm because I didn't want to alarm my husband.

Finally I could stand it no longer. I left James's bedside, locked myself in the bathroom, and cried convulsively. I prayed as hard as I knew, using words from the depths of my soul, and begged the Lord to spare my husband from cancer. As I prayed, I found myself trying hopelessly to douse the tiny sparks of doubt that had somehow ignited a little fire that I was battling feverishly to put out. What if my people were wrong? What if Jesus is God? What if Jesus really is the Messiah of Israel? What if I need to acknowledge Jesus in my prayer? To cover all my bases, I hastily added, "And Jesus, if you are really there, and you are who James says you are, I'm asking you too." I regained my composure, washed my face, unlocked the door, and returned to my husband.

I stayed in the hospital that day until it grew so dark outside that James insisted I go home. Again I made the hour-long drive up the coast all alone. I drank a glass of milk and got ready for bed. But I couldn't sleep.

Who in the world was Jesus? Was I right or was James right? How could a man possibly be God? How could there be three gods—Father, Son, and Holy Spirit—or, as James described it, one God in three persons. That concept alone tore at the very heart of monotheistic Judaism, whose creedal statement is the *Shema* of Deuteronomy 6:4: "HEAR, O ISRAEL: THE LORD OUR GOD, THE LORD IS ONE" (Masoretic Text). The idea of worshiping Jesus just screamed out *goyishe, goyishe* (gentile, gentile). I was not a *goy*. I was a Jew, and the baby I was carrying was also a Jew.

I thought of my people and all they had suffered at the hands of the Gentiles, and I felt like a traitor for having even thought about Jesus. What would my parents have said? They had sacrificed so much to make sure I received a Jewish education because they wanted me to know where I belonged and how to live as a Jew. Consumed with guilt, I sat alone on my bed and cried. I begged the Lord to forgive me for having addressed Jesus, and through my tears, I made a vow. "I promise you," I said aloud, "that this baby I'm carrying will be a Jew; and as long as I live, it will never worship anyone but the God of Abraham, Isaac, and Jacob." Then I fell asleep.

The results of the myelogram arrived the following day. A slipped disk! No tumor. No cancer. No life-threatening illness. The disk was pressing on a nerve, producing my husband's excruciating leg pain. I was relieved beyond description. The hastily scheduled surgery was just as hastily canceled, and the doctors settled on treating James with traction followed by complete rest. Two weeks later he was discharged. A slender man to begin with, he had lost so much weight in the hospital that he could barely cinch his belt tight enough to keep his pants from falling down. When the identical incident recurred two years later, he saw a good chiropractor and walked out of the office the same night feeling 100 percent better.

My prayers had been answered. Life returned to normal, for which I profusely thanked the God of my people Israel and tried to blot from memory my brief transgression into the territory of the Gentiles. Soon August rolled around and I gave birth to my firstborn, a beautiful baby girl whom we named Jamie Rae after my husband (James) and my mother (Rae).

Four months later James changed jobs. He assumed the vice presidency of a newspaper in New Jersey and we prepared to leave the sunny South. My husband left immediately, and I was to stay behind with Jamie until our house sold. However, two weeks into his job, James told me the company was offering me a position customizing and installing the software for a computerized phototypesetting system it had ordered. Was I interested?

Was I interested! He was talking to the only girl in junior high who wanted to take shop instead of cooking. Not that I could. In those days, if you wore a skirt, you had to wear an apron too. By the end of seventh grade I had finally mastered applesauce, and by the end of eighth, I had added to my meager repertoire some gloppy white stuff studded with green peas and tuna. Cooking eluded me. I couldn't cook anything Southern. I couldn't cook anything Jewish. I could barely cook anything American. To this day I am amazed that anyone would title a book *The Joy of Cooking*. As far as I was concerned, there was only one thing I disliked more—fishing.

My husband, in truth, was a far better cook than I was. And when I asked him to name the women he considered to be among the best cooks he'd ever known, he sealed forever the little lid on my crockpot of motivation. He told me his mother (particularly when she was young) and his ex-wife.

So I happily returned to work. I commuted to New Jersey, leaving my four-month-old daughter in the capable hands of a grandmotherly, experienced, live-in nurse who took expert care of her. For many months I worked in New Jersey during the week and flew home to Florida on weekends. It was a tiresome arrangement, and I missed Jamie terribly.

It was during this time, however, that I went to Sacramento, California. I needed a week of training with the computer corporation building our phototypesetting system. It provided the perfect opportunity to visit Nancy. Although we spoke regularly on the telephone, we had not seen each other since my wedding, and I was looking forward to a reunion with my oldest and dearest friend.

Nancy lived in Orange County. She picked me up at the airport in Los Angeles, and it felt as though we had never been apart. Although we had less than twenty-four hours together before I had to fly to Sacramento, we were determined to make the most of it. She introduced me to some of her friends, chauffeured me around the area, and filled me in on her new job and the man she was dating. I filled her in on our hunt for a house, on my job, my husband, and my baby daughter. It was good to be together again, and it was good to be back in California. When I had been single I had spent many wonderful months there installing a system, and I had a treasure trove of fond memories.

Nancy and I did much catching up. In the morning we decided to go for brunch before I went north. As we sat across the table, the subject of religion came up. To Nancy, I was Mrs. Jewish. This was the woman who had once told me, "You're so Jewish, you should've been a rabbi." Surprisingly, she did not register any shock when I told her I was pondering the possibility that the Jewish people might possibly be wrong about Jesus.

"According to the Scriptures, we're *often* wrong," I told her in tones of frustration and disappointment. "What if we've been wrong about this too?"

Nancy sat there and said nothing. Apart from my husband, she understood me better than any person alive. She knew my fierce loyalty to Judaism, my strong identification with my Jewish heritage, and she grasped immediately the magnitude of the struggle that had begun within me.

"How am I ever going to find out the truth?" I asked. I didn't know. It seemed a hopeless quest. I dropped the subject and went back to the buffet table, aware that I might not have another chance to eat that day.

Our time together drew to a close. We returned to Nancy's home so I could gather my things and go to the airport in Los Angeles. As I stood in the bedroom packing, Nancy walked in, closed the door, sat on the bed, and told me to sit down.

"Lorna," she said. "I have something to tell you."

"What is it?" I asked.

"I've become a Christian."

Now it was my turn not to be shocked. Nor was I disgusted, offended, or angry—all the ways I would have reacted earlier. Only a year ago, I had heard a Jewish man on television talk about Jesus being the Messiah, and I had considered him such a contemptible traitor that I happily would have stoned him, given the chance. But for some reason, I did not feel that way now. I did not feel like ranting or raving or exploding at Nancy or demanding to know how she could have committed such a heinous crime.

Instead, I found myself welcoming this news as a fortuitous turn of events. Finally there was someone I trusted who not only understood me and my perspective but who also might shed some light on this person named Jesus.

"What do you mean?" I asked.

"I've asked Jesus to be my personal Savior."

"What do you mean?" I asked again, baffled by the strange terminology. "You're not one of those *born-again* Christians, are you?"

"Yes," she said. "I am. I wasn't going to tell you, but after you said what you did in the restaurant, I felt I could. I've been praying for you, Lorna."

I could tell that she was different. Something had happened to her on the inside that was manifesting itself on the outside. She was excited about what she had found and exhibited a peace and contentment that I had never seen in her before. And never once had I ever known her to pray.

"Explain it to me," I asked. "What happened?"

Nancy worked in a hospital in those days. A nurse named Elaine had befriended her and had talked to her many times about Jesus. Elaine, Nancy said, explained why Jesus came to earth, what He had accomplished, and how God requires men to respond to Him. Nancy said Elaine gave her many books to read, and after a year of reading, she concluded that Elaine was right. Jesus was God. He had died for her sins; and she had asked Him to become her Savior.

"But what convinced you?" I asked.

First, she pointed out that both *Elohim* and *Adonai*, Hebrew names of God that I had used all my life, are plural. There is only one God—the God of Israel—she told me. However, He is a compound unity composed of Father, Son, and Holy Spirit. I learned much later that the *Shema* even allows for this: "HEAR, O ISRAEL: THE LORD OUR GOD, THE LORD IS ONE" (Dt. 6:4, Masoretic Text.)

The word *one* is the Hebrew word *echad*, which often denotes two or more things that come together to form a single unit. In Genesis 2, for example, God put Adam and Eve together and declared them to be "one" flesh (Gen.

2:24). Obviously they were still two separate human beings, but they had become *echad,* a compound unity that formed a perfect whole.

Jesus, said Nancy, is the second person of a three-part, unified Godhead. He came to earth to be the Messiah promised to the Jewish people. He came to be a sacrificial lamb who would bear our sins and take our punishment. Because He was deity, He was sinless—without spot and without blemish. That made him a perfect and acceptable sacrifice for a holy and a righteous God.

His death, she said, satisfied God's requirement that blood be shed to obtain forgiveness of sin. His shed blood makes it possible for every human being on earth to receive forgiveness from God, but each person must individually request that forgiveness of God by faith.

It made sense, but I was not able to believe it.

When a person was sent to jail in the days of the Romans, Nancy explained, the list of his offenses were written up and nailed to his cell door. After serving his time, the prisoner was released. The list of offenses was removed from the door, stamped "paid in full," and handed to him so he could forever prove that he had paid the price for his crimes and could never be jailed for the same offenses again.

"Jesus paid the price for all of us," she said. "It's as though our offenses were nailed to his cross. He did the time, and our sins have been 'paid in full.' You just have to believe that and ask Him to be your Savior."

I understood the concept, but how could I verify its truth? Why should I trust Christian theology any more than Jewish theology? What proof was there? Where was the corroboration? Nancy had given me something to think about, but I needed more. How was I ever going to find out what was true? One thing was certain, though. I knew by now that somehow I had to.

We said our good-byes at the airport and I flew to Sacramento. All I could think about on the airplane was our conversation about Jesus. However, so much evil has been done to the Jewish people in that name. How, I thought, could Jesus possibly be the Messiah? It did not make sense. Yet Judaism's casual dismissal of the need for blood sacrifice did not make sense either. Hadn't God said in Malachi 3:6 "I am the LORD, I change not?" If God had required sacrifice during the days of Moses and the periods of Temple history, why would He change and not require it now? What in the world was true? "Oh God," I prayed, "you're going to have to help me."

That night in the hotel, I tried to watch television but was too restless and could not. I tried to sleep, but Nancy's explanation kept running through my mind. Finally I turned on the light. "I know there are usually Bibles in hotel rooms," I thought. "There must be one here." I leaned over, opened the drawer of my nightstand, and sure enough, there lay a Bible that had been placed by The Gideons International. In all my life I had never seen a New Testament. Almost afraid of bringing down the wrath of God if I read it, I leafed carefully through the pages. Then I remembered my Uncle Saul having told me that he had once read the New Testament. If *he* had read it, I thought, it must be safe to read.

So I began at the beginning.

> *The book of the genealogy of Jesus Christ, the son of David, the son of Abraham. Abraham begot Isaac; and Isaac begot Jacob; and Jacob begot Judah and his brethren; And Judah begot Perez and Zerah of Tamar . . .* (Mt. 1:1–3).

Oh No! The begats. I hated the begats! The Hebrew
Scriptures are filled with them and they go on and on and
on. No sense boring myself with those, I decided. So I
moved on. I tried the Gospel of John.

> *In the beginning was the Word, and the Word was*
> *with God, and the Word was God. The same was*
> *in the beginning with God. All things were made*
> *by him; and without him was not anything made*
> *that was made. In him was life; and the life was*
> *the light of men. And the light shineth in dark-*
> *ness; and the darkness overcame [comprehended]*
> *it not* (Jn. 1:1–5).

What in the world did that mishmash mean? "How do
people understand this stuff?" I thought. So I moved on
again. I read about my sheep and these sheep and those
sheep and some other sheep, and I had no idea whose
sheep any of the sheep were. I was in John chapter 10 and
thoroughly confused. But for some reason I felt compelled
to keep reading. Finally I arrived at verse 22:

> *And it was at Jerusalem the feast of the dedication*
> *[Hanukkah], and it was winter. And Jesus*
> *walked in the temple in Solomon's porch. Then*
> *came the Jews round about him, and said unto*
> *him, How long dost thou make us to doubt? If*
> *thou be the Christ [Messiah], tell us plainly.*
> *Jesus answered them, I told you, and ye believed*
> *not; the works that I do in my Father's name, they*
> *bear witness of me. . . . If I do not the works of my*
> *Father, believe me not. But if I do, though ye*
> *believe not me, believe the works, that ye may*
> *know, and believe, that the Father is in me, and I*
> *in him* (Jn. 10:22–25, 37–38).

Miraculously, something clicked. I understood what was being said. Jesus was telling the Jewish leaders that they should be able to figure out who He is by what He does. If they did not believe what He said about himself, they could ascertain if He was telling the truth by examining His works.

Suddenly I knew what I had to do. I had to stop dwelling on all the evil that had been done to my people in Jesus' name and examine Jesus himself. I had to investigate the works of Jesus. However, that was easier said than done. I did not own a New Testament and did not intend to buy one, particularly since I felt I would never be able to understand it anyway. But the idea stayed with me.

After my week in Sacramento, I returned to New Jersey, and life almost overwhelmed me with activity. We closed on a house and soon were able to bring Jamie home from down South. Now I was a working mother with a new home to get in order and an extremely demanding job that required I hire a nanny. Life was busy indeed.

Somehow I still found time to entertain two people from the computer company in Sacramento. They were the specialists sent out to get our system running. James had invited them to dinner. As we sat in the living room and talked, up popped the subject of God.

John, the senior specialist, was an atheist. He didn't believe in the existence of God and, in his cerebral manner, argued that even if there were a God, He wouldn't care about human beings any more than He would care about the bark on trees or the mud on your shoes. Mary, the other specialist, was a Catholic. She believed there was a God, but she was no match for John. James, the Baptist, carried the ball. He said he not only believed in God but also made a case for God's love for man.

Finally John looked at my husband and said, "James, you talk as though you know God personally."

James replied very matter-of-factly, "That's because I do."

During the entire discussion, I sat there like a bump on a log.

"What do you believe?" John asked me, knowing I was not usually so unopinionated. This subject, however, had silenced me. I knew now that I no longer knew what I believed.

"I'm Jewish," I said, "and I definitely believe there's a God. But right now I don't know what I believe about Jesus. I've been wondering if perhaps the Jewish people have been wrong."

The discussion changed to something else, but now I was plagued all over again. What I had tried desperately to shove aside and forget had shot to the forefront once more. Who was Jesus? What was the truth?

Several days later I called Nancy. "What do I do?" I asked. "What can I read? I have to have some answers."

Nancy told me to read the Gospel of John. I asked my husband if he owned a Bible. Not five minutes later he produced a black leather King James Bible with his name engraved on it. So I began again. I did not understand a word, but this time I was determined to read the entire book of John even if it killed me.

> *Verily, verily, I say unto thee, Except a man be born again, he cannot see the kingdom of God. . . . Except a man be born of water and of the Spirit, he cannot enter into the kingdom of God. That which is born of the flesh is flesh; and that which is born of the Spirit is spirit. Marvel not that I said unto thee, Ye must be born again* (Jn. 3:3, 5–7).

More double-talk. Well, at least I had located the term "born again," even though I still had no idea what it meant.

How in the world could a person be born a second time after he was born once already? But I kept going. Then I hit it—or rather, it hit me: John 3:16. The verse penetrated the very center of my being. I stared at it, reading it over and over again.

> For God so loved the world, that he gave his only begotten Son, that whosoever believeth in him should not perish, but have everlasting life.

I must have reread the verse twenty times. Then I inserted my own name and read it aloud: "For God so loved Lorna that he gave his only begotten Son, that if Lorna believes in him, Lorna should not perish, but have everlasting life." All my life no one had ever told me that God loved me. This verse said that God actually loved me so much that He sent His Son to die for *me*. Could God actually love *me* that much? I thought of all the wrong things I had done in my life. Yet God loved me? What a deep, unfathomable love that would be, if it were true. A person could endure great heartache in peace with a love like that.

Then I thought of Mrs. Bennett. This was the love she believed God had for her. She trusted in it and had built her life around it. She believed that God loved her so much that He had sent his son to die for her personally; and she clung to the promise that "whosoever believeth in him should not perish, but have everlasting life."

He sent His son to die for *me*. His *son*, I thought. How did I know it was true? Someone could have made it up. How would I ever be able to find the truth? I wanted desperately to believe that God loved me, but I did not trust the Gentile Bible. So I cried out to the God of Abraham, Isaac, and Jacob, begging Him to show me the truth. Then I called Nancy.

"What was the one thing you read that helped you the most?" I asked. I remembered that it had taken her a year of reading and searching before she had accepted Jesus as God and Messiah. "I don't have a year," I said. "If I have to wait that long, I'll end up insane. What was the one book you read that clinched it for you?" She told me to get *The Liberation of Planet Earth* by Hal Lindsay.

So I drove to the mall. "Never heard of it," replied the clerk in bookstore number one. I asked her to check her catalogs and see if she could order it.

"Do you know who publishes it?" she said.

No, I did not. On to bookstore number two, then to number three. I tried every bookstore for miles, and no one had ever heard of *The Liberation of Planet Earth*. The store clerks thought it was about an alien invasion. When I told them it was a religious book, they just shook their heads and said, "We don't carry many of that type." Then I went to the public library; but no one there had ever heard of it either. By now I was becoming frantic. Somehow I had to find this book.

The month was December 1980. Christmas was coming, and we were getting ready to go to North Carolina to be with the family. How I treasured those trips. Well, I didn't really treasure the *trip*—I treasured the destination at the end of the trip. The trips were almost unbearable. Neither James nor I liked driving, so we took turns. He drove two hours, then I drove two hours, so on and so forth, until eleven hours later we finally parked the car in Mrs. Bennett's driveway, went into the kitchen, and took some Excedrin.

But it was always worth it, especially at Christmas time. When we arrived, the tree was up, the decorations were on, the house was buzzing with activity, and the telephone was ringing off the hook. James's older sister, a widow herself, had driven in from Wilmington to be there to greet us. She and my mother-in-law embraced us with joy, then quickly scooped Jamie up in delight. James strolled into the kitchen and snooped in all the pots on the stove like a little boy who was eagerly anticipating the prospect of eating some good cooking. Laughter and hugs and a warmth of spirit pervaded the entire house. In short, there was no place I would rather have been.

As Christmas Eve drew closer, James's married daughter asked if I wanted to do some last-minute shopping at the Myrtle Beach Mall in South Carolina. It was only a short drive, and she still had some things she wanted to get for her husband. So off we went. Since I had never been to that mall before, I roamed around surveying the terrain. Suddenly a sign caught my attention. It read "Christian Bookstore." A Christian bookstore! I could not believe it! I never knew such a thing existed. Maybe someone here will have heard of *The Liberation of Planet Earth.*

"I do think we have that book," said the salesgirl. "It's back here."

I practically held my breath as I followed her to the very back of the store, but we didn't see it anywhere. Then, as if by magic, she removed from the shelf a completely unrelated book bearing a completely different title, and directly behind it sat the store's one-and-only copy of *The Liberation of Planet Earth* by Hal Lindsay (Bantam Books).

Finally! I bought it. My stepdaughter and I walked around a little more then headed home. If I bought anything else that trip, I don't remember it. I just remember clutching that little book as though its pages had been made of purest gold. "Oh Lord," I said, "please let it have the answers I need. Please, just show me the truth."

For the next several days, I sat on the living room couch reading. Somehow I blotted out all the activity taking place around me; and like Mary and her little lamb, everywhere I went, the book was sure to go. First, I remember being struck by the fact that Lindsay had an incredible grasp of the Hebrew Scriptures and exhibited a profound appreciation for Jewish things. How odd in a Gentile, I thought. Then I was struck by the teaching.

He explained the creation account in the book of Genesis in a way that made complete and logical sense. God had created a perfect and orderly universe where everything reproduced after its own kind. That's why, to this day, cherry trees always reproduce cherry trees, orange trees yield more orange trees, dogs give birth to dogs, cats to cats, monkeys to monkeys, and human beings always just reproduce other human beings. So much for evolution.

Adam and Eve were singularly distinct from the rest of God's creation. They alone were created "in the image of God." They possessed the abilities to think and reason logically, to discipline themselves to live on a higher plane than that of pure instinct; and they had the free will to make conscious decisions concerning the paths their lives would take. Unfortunately, early on they made the wrong decisions.

Eve, succumbing to deception, sinned by disobeying God, then prompted her husband to do the same. Adam, however, disobeyed with his eyes wide open. He knew exactly what he was doing, did it willingly and in complete defiance of his Creator. Thus Adam became a sinner. He went his own way instead of God's way simply because it was the way he wanted to go. Since the father carries the seed, he transmits the sin nature. Thus Adam transmitted his propensity for evil to every child he fathered; and his sons passed it on to their children, so on and so forth, right up to the present day. Just as a cherry tree only reproduces other cherry trees, so can a sinner only reproduce other sinners.

For the first time, I understood the root of anti-Semitism. While growing up, I had often heard it said that man was basically good. Yet reality showed me differently. If man were basically good, how did you explain something as evil as the Holocaust? If man were basically good, how did you explain the pogroms and the Spanish Inquisition? If man were basically good, how did you explain the fact that even little children on a school playground can be so mean and hateful that their actions long ago gave rise to the proverb "children can be so cruel"?

I had been a history major in college. I knew well that the annals of human endeavor were not filled with love, compassion, and the milk of human kindness. Instead, they were satiated with blood, wars, violence, hatred, brutality, and self-ambition. My years in journalism, covering history in the making, only confirmed that fact. Now I finally understood why. Sin! As God had explained through the prophet Jeremiah, "The heart is deceitful above all things, and desperately wicked" (Jer. 17:9).

After completing His creation, a perfect, holy, and righteous God had pronounced everything "good." Then man messed it all up. No wonder the God of Israel always seemed to be railing against sin. It appeared to be His number one priority. Now I knew why. Our sinfulness pervades everything. It eats away at our lives and our society like a cancer. It prevents us from obeying the *Shema*: "And thou shalt love the LORD thy God with all thine heart, and with all thy soul, and with all thy might" (Dt. 6:5, Masoretic Text). It prevents us from emulating Him and, consequently, from leading lives of righteousness out of love for Him, to bring glory and honor to His holy Name.

This was the cold, hard truth. It is the bad news about mankind that mankind doesn't like to face. Perhaps that is why H. L. Mencken wrote, "What remains in the world . . . is a series of long-tested and solidly agreeable lies." But lies are like anesthesia: They don't change the facts. They just numb you and dull you so you cannot see the facts or respond to them. Yet it is the truth that sets us free; and the truth is that there is good news too.

God has provided a way of escape. A repentant sinner can receive a new heart and forgiveness of sin through a conversion experience—an inward change that God had revealed through the prophet Ezekiel: "A new heart also will I give you, and a new spirit will I put within you; and I will take away the stony heart out of your flesh, and I will give you an heart of flesh" (Ezek. 36:26).

As King David himself had written, "Create in me a clean heart, O God, and renew a right spirit within me. . . . Then will I teach transgressors thy ways, and sinners shall be **converted** [emphasis added] unto thee" (Ps. 51:10, 13).

Suddenly everything became clear. It was as though the pieces of a giant and mysterious puzzle all took their appropriate places, forming a beautiful portrait of a love so deep, a love so unbelievable that I sat on my mother-in-law's couch and cried. God loved me! In fact, He loved me so much that He had come to earth Himself in the person of Jesus more than two thousand years ago to willingly bear my sin and become my sacrifice. Just as the ancient Israelites had brought their offerings to the Temple, placed their hands upon the heads of the innocent animals, and symbolically transferred their sins to the heads of the lambs to be slain, so had God transferred my sin, once and for all, to the head of Messiah Jesus. Then I read the New Testament verse of Hebrews 9:12: "Neither by the blood of goats and calves, but by his own blood he entered in once into the holy place, having obtained eternal redemption for us."

Finally I grasped the crucial necessity of the virgin birth. If Jesus were to be a sinbearer, He could not possibly have had an earthly father, because then Jesus would have been a sinner, just like me, and an unfit sacrifice.

Jesus *had* to be God because only God is perfect, without sin. The sacrifice had to be perfect. However, God cannot die. That is why He needed a mortal body that could taste death, why He could rise from the dead, and why He will come again someday to restore the Davidic Kingdom to my people and reign on the throne of King David of Israel forever.

I knew now that animal blood never was intended to *remove* the sin of man, just to *cover* it temporarily. Thus animal sacrifices had to be repeated over and over again. They were temporary until the time was right for the perfect sacrifice to be made, once for all. That perfect sacrifice was the Messiah of Israel, who died to remove the sins not only of Jewish people, but of people everywhere—Jew and Gentile alike. But each individual has to appropriate that knowledge for himself by faith.

Then, at the moment we believe, God Himself "converts" us. He gives us a new heart and stamps our sin debt "paid in full."

It was not enough to believe that Jesus "died for the sins of the world," as I had heard from my Gentile friends while I was growing up. The point was not that He had died for everyone. The point was that He had died for ME.

It does not matter if you are born Jewish, Baptist, Catholic, Muslim, or whatever. There is only one God—the God of Abraham, Isaac, and Jacob. And there is only one way to obtain forgiveness of sin from that God and receive the free gift of eternal life that goes with it: by placing your faith in the death and resurrection of Jesus (*Yeshua* in Hebrew)—the second person of a unified, triune Godhead—the Jewish Messiah of Israel, the only Redeemer of humanity. As God Himself had declared through the prophet Isaiah,

> *Thus saith the* LORD, *the King of Israel,* **and his redeemer** *[emphasis added], the* LORD *of hosts: I am the first, and I am the last, and beside me there is no God* (Isa. 44:6).

There it was. That very verse in the Hebrew Scriptures showed the first and second persons of a triune God. Everything made sense. In an instant I understood inconsistencies in religious teaching that had plagued me all my life. Now I knew why God had allowed the Temple to be destroyed in A.D. 70. We didn't need it! The final sacrifice had been made! A holy God demanded the ultimate price be paid to obtain forgiveness of sin. Yet in His profound and incomprehensible love for me, He had paid that price Himself.

Later I learned that God had told my people more than seven hundred years before the birth of Jesus that Messiah would be a sacrifice for sin.

> *But he was wounded for our transgressions, he was bruised for our iniquities; the chastisement for our peace was upon him, and with his stripes we are healed. All we like sheep have gone astray; we have turned every one to his own way, and the* LORD *hath laid on him the iniquity of us all* (Isa. 53:5–6).

At last I understood. There was no heavenly scale upon which God weighed my good deeds against my bad. God was far more merciful. He had taken all my bad, had laid them on the head of my Redeemer, and had punished Jesus instead of me. No matter how many good deeds you rack up in this lifetime, no matter how decently you try to live, no matter how sincerely you try to follow the Golden Rule, none of these things can remove sin. Only God can remove sin, and He only does it if you ask Him to, by faith. Nothing more. "For whosoever shall call upon the name of the Lord shall be saved" (Rom. 10:13).

And no amount of good deeds can make you a part of God's family any more than they can make you a part of your earthly father's family. You were born into the latter, and you have to be born *again* into the former. Birth, that's what does it—a new, spiritual birth that produces a new heart.

So the first chance I had, I got down on my knees, confessed my sin, and asked the Lord Jesus Christ—the God and Hope of my people Israel—to become my Messiah and to remove my sin with His blood. Finally, at thirty-one years old, I had been set free.

Chapter Four

☙

The Big Red Crayon

All of life seemed different to me now—more lucid and comprehensible. I had finally found the truth; and it gave me peace, stability, purpose, and direction. Yes, God loved me. He had answered my prayers, He had forgiven my sins, and He had imparted to me His wondrous gift of life everlasting. The God who had divided the Red Sea for Moses was the same God who, I knew now, lovingly held my breath in His hand and charted all my tomorrows. From now throughout eternity, I belonged to the Lord Jesus, and He belonged to me. I knew for sure that when I closed my eyes for the last time, I would awake in the presence of the God of Abraham, Isaac, and Jacob.

Hallelujah! I had my ticket to heaven, and it was stamped and ready to go, just like my mother-in-law's. The Lord Jesus had bought it for me with His blood, and now I had collected it, by faith. I literally owed the Lord

Jesus my life and wanted to learn as much about Him and my new faith as I could.

That meant going to church. Although I had not really gotten to know the area very well over the past year, I knew there was a big church only three blocks from our house. So I asked James if he wanted to go on Sunday. He missed going to church but had never mentioned if for fear of appearing that he was pressuring me into doing something I didn't want to do. So in January 1981 we went to church for the first time since we moved to New Jersey.

As we entered the large vestibule, the first thing I noticed was an illuminated sign above the doors leading into the sanctuary, announcing with dignified simplicity, "On the Air." It turned out that the morning worship service was broadcasted live each Sunday over radio station WCHR-FM in Trenton.

The place was bustling. As we took our seats, the choir began to sing. All at once I was overcome with a love for God that was rooted in the profound reality of His presence, His mercy, and His lovingkindness. His presence enveloped me completely, giving me a peace and contentment I had never known. The choir's call to worship sounded to me like the music of heaven. I cried through the entire service. I still did not know a single hymn; but every word we sang expressed precisely what I was feeling, and I thanked God over and over for having shown me the truth. I felt like the most fortunate Jewish person in the world. Without hesitation, I filled out a visitor's card and indicated that I wanted to be baptized.

The next evening, our doorbell rang. A couple from the church's Monday night visitation team had been given the card I had filled out and stopped by. Gladys and Don, James and I sat in the living room for hours and talked. So far the only one who knew about my new birth was Nancy. I had not even told my husband. Evidently, James had perceived what had happened. But Don and Gladys were uncertain because I didn't use any of the standard Christian jargon to explain my new relationship with God. I had only been saved three weeks. I didn't know any jargon. Finally, my husband looked at me and said, "Lorna, I think you'd better tell them the whole story, including your background." So I did.

They, in turn, told me about the new believers' Sunday school class and the Tuesday ladies' Bible study at the church, with a nursery for Jamie. The next morning, when the church doors opened, I was there.

To my knowledge, none of the thirty or so women who attended the Bible study had a clue who I was, and I certainly did not know a single one of them. They seemed like nice ladies—many of them my age. However, their vocabulary was peppered with words I didn't understand, such as *witnessing* and *fellowshipping*. They had all brought their Bibles. I didn't even own one, and I certainly did not know the books of the New Testament.

After about ten minutes, I deduced that *fellowshipping* must be a Christian buzz word akin to "socializing." So far so good. *Witnessing*, however, had me stumped. In my realm of understanding, all these ladies had either seen a whole lot of car accidents or had spent too much time in court. No matter how I tried, I could not formulate a contextually accurate definition.

Finally I raised my hand. All eyes turned in my direction. No matter, I was determined to ask my question. Asking questions, after all, had been my business, even when it meant butting into someone else's business. And I knew that wasn't the case here.

"Excuse me," I said. "But what does *witnessing* mean?"

Someone very graciously explained that it means telling others about your faith in the Lord Jesus.

"Oh, thank you," I replied, not feeling the least bit uncomfortable for some reason. As a matter of fact, it seemed that from then on, all the women went out of their way to be friendly. At the end of the Bible study, one woman my age, also with a child in the nursery, introduced herself and inquired about my background. I almost fell over when she beamed with delight over the fact that I was Jewish. Still remembering my father's stern admonition, "you'll never be accepted by the *goyim*," I had decided not to reveal my Jewishness to anyone. Somehow, though, telling her had become unavoidable.

"Are you doing anything right now?" she asked. "Would you like to come over for lunch?" So Jamie and I went home with Marilyn, and that afternoon, the Lord laid the foundation for what was to become one of my closest and most cherished friendships for many years.

The following Sunday I began attending the new believers' class that met for an hour prior to the worship service. Approximately ten of us sat around a long table. We had two teachers. One was a kind, gentle, dedicated man of God named Bob Beveridge, who was to become a dear friend, praying for me every day without fail for years. The other was a perky, extremely knowledgeable 63-year-old woman named Mae Cheatle, who exemplified all the qualities of someone who had walked with the Lord for many years. I took to her right away. Everyone but Bob and Mae were brand-new Christians. I was the only one, however, who had come from a Jewish background. Again, I hesitated to reveal that fact, but it inevitably escaped.

To my astonishment, Mae reacted just as Marilyn had. Not only was she thrilled, but she also told me she would not be surprised if God actually suited a special blessing to Jewish people who got saved because we were His Chosen People. Incredible! I could not believe what I was hearing! A Gentile was calling the Jewish people "God's Chosen People." I was amazed; but what amazed me even more was that everyone at this church seemed to feel the same way, including the pastor.

All the messages from the pulpit of Dr. David W. Allen taught the Bible in a surprisingly Jewish context. He talked about a time when God would regather Israel and restore to them the Kingdom of David, with Messiah Jesus reigning on the throne. He took texts from the Old Testament, then from the New Testament, and taught them as one cohesive, unified whole. I was stunned at how precisely they went together and how the ancient prophecies that had dumbfounded me in Hebrew school now made perfect sense. Everything fit like a hand in a glove, just as Bob Ferm had told me when I had first met him in his study in Florida. The people in this church had more faith in God's love for the Jewish people and in the promises God had made to us than my people had themselves.

When Tuesday rolled around again, I returned to the ladies' Bible study. There I met two more women who became very dear friends. One invited me to go with her to the Christian Women's Club luncheon the following day. She picked me up at home, and we drove to the restaurant. Almost two hundred women laughed, *fellowshipped*, and thoroughly enjoyed themselves for what seemed like the shortest two and one-half hours in memory. There was music, an interesting program, a delicious lunch, hilarious announcements inviting everyone to return next month, and then a speaker who told about her search for God and how she had become a Christian. When the speaker was finished, she prayed, extending an invitation to all the women in the audience to receive the Lord Jesus as personal Savior.

How amazing, I thought, that the vast majority of Gentiles in the world, many of whom had grown up in church all their lives, still were not Christians. Becoming a Christian required a conversion of the heart—a new birth. It required humbling yourself to the very point of realizing that nothing you do in this lifetime can clean you up enough to stand before a holy God; and it required trusting not in your good deeds but in the Lord Jesus alone to remove your sin. My mother-in-law, a life-long Baptist, had become a Christian at age fifteen, when she "got converted." I had become one at thirty-one. There I sat, the only Jewish woman in a room full of Gentiles, and it dawned on me how unbelievable yet altogether marvelous it was that I was one of the redeemed.

Had anyone ever told me just a year earlier that a Jewish person could be both a Jew and a Christian at the same time, I would have laughed in his face. But it is true. The term *Christian* simply means "follower of Christ." The word *Christ* comes from the Greek word *Cristos*, which in Hebrew is *Mashiach*, or "Messiah" in English. A *Christian*, therefore, be he Jewish or Gentile, is nothing more than a "follower of Messiah." What could possibly be more appropriate for a Jew than to be a follower of the Jewish Messiah?

Appropriate, yes. Easy, no. During the first six weeks of my new life, despite all the Bible teaching I was absorbing, despite the multitude of blessing that the Lord was cascading down on me, I still struggled with guilt. I felt like a traitor to my people. It helped somewhat that I now understood that most of the hatred and persecution that had dogged the Jewish people down through the ages had come not from true Christians but from unconverted Gentiles. But I still encountered guilt. Every day I begged the Lord to remove it; but He did not. Finally I called Nancy.

"Read the book of Romans," she told me. "I think that's what you need."

I still had no Bible of my own, so I took James's and began with Romans chapter 1. In less than five minutes, God had spoken to me:

> For I am not ashamed of the gospel of Christ; for it is the power of God unto salvation to everyone that believeth; to the Jew first, and also to the Greek [Gentile] (Rom.1:16).

"Oh God," I screamed aloud. "Thank you, thank you, thank you!" Belief in Christ was what He had wanted all along for His Chosen People! He had even offered salvation through the Lord Jesus to us first, then to the Gentiles. In becoming a Hebrew Christian—a Jewish follower of Messiah, or a Messianic Jew—I was doing what God wanted *all* Jews to do: to place our complete faith and trust in Him and in His Redeemer. I had come full circle. I was a *completed* Jew. I finally understood what that term meant! And for the first time in my life, I got down on my knees and thanked the Lord that I had been born a Jew.

By now Jamie was sixteen months old. Mercifully, my job had ended four months earlier, and I was home with my daughter. Every time she took a nap, I grabbed James's Bible, settled myself into a rocking chair, and read. I devoured it for hours each day, and I marveled at how easy it was to understand now. First I read the four Gospels and wept over the actual physical torture the Lord Jesus had endured to redeem me. I began talking to Him constantly about everything. I talked to Him when I was driving in my car, when I was peeling potatoes, when I was lying in bed, when I was alone, and when I was in the midst of hundreds of people. I reveled in the fact that I knew He heard my every word, including the silent meditations of my heart. But best of all, now He talked to me.

Through the Word of God, the Lord revealed His thoughts to me. Sometimes He told me how He wanted me to behave, what my priorities should be, what I should flee, and what I should cling to. Sometimes He pointed out areas in my life that He needed to take control of. Sometimes He gently corrected me. Sometimes He reproved me. But always, always, He told me He loved me.

I became a regular at Christian Women's Club. I attended the luncheon each month, two Christian Women's Club Bible studies each week, the church Bible study every Tuesday morning, Sunday school, plus Sunday morning and evening worship. Each week I memorized a typed sheet of verses that Mae handed out in Sunday school. And in time, I even began to understand some of the terminology associated with my new faith: justification, sanctification, propitiation, conviction, regeneration, Rapture of the church, Great Tribulation, premillenial, pretribulational, the Time of Jacob's Trouble, etc.

One week in Sunday school, Mae suggested that anyone who had been used of God to lead us to salvation probably would like to know about it. So that week I wrote two letters: one to Mrs. Bennett and one to Bob and Lois Ferm, who by then had moved back to their home in Asheville, North Carolina. They were all thrilled to hear my news. Not long afterward, Mrs. Bennett bought me a beautiful leather Bible of my very own. Bob wrote back, and he and Lois became even more precious to me as the years went by. I stayed in touch with Bob until his death in 1993 and am in touch with Lois to this day. What choice servants of the Most High God had He put in my path.

The majority of my closest friends, however, came from Christian Women's Club. It drew its workers from churches all across town. Before I knew it, I was asked to serve on the Executive Board as Life Publications chairman. "That will be okay," I thought, "as long as I never have to get in front of the microphone." The idea of addressing two hundred women for any reason at all terrified me. I was assured that all I would have to do would be to stand behind a table and sell the little Life Publication booklets. No sooner had I taken the job, however, than my dear friend Jean, who was to become like a mother to me, decided it was time we had a Life Publications announcement.

Now, announcements at the luncheon had a life all their own. For the most part, they were executed with great gusto, in pomp and fanfare and costume, accompanied by all the commotion of a Broadway production. Sometimes they went awry, but that made them all the more hilarious; and the women absolutely loved them. One month the board member whose job it was to announce the following month's luncheon decided to dress like a country girl down on the farm. Daintily toting a basket of eggs on her arm, she skipped up to the microphone and placed on the head table a big box that she explained, with appropriate Southern drawl, contained a chicken.

Sitting at the head table was the chairman of the Executive Board, a veteran of Club herself, who had rendered her own share of bizarre announcements. Even *she* did not believe anyone would actually bring a live chicken to the luncheon. So while "country girl" detailed the slate of upcoming events, the chairman slightly pried open the lid of the box, discretely trying to peek inside. In a flash, out flew a chicken. It soared from the carton flapping its wings furiously over the heads of two hundred shrieking women who, between screams, managed to voice their downright astonishment that chickens could actually fly. Periodically the bird would light on the floor, clucking its way under tables as terrified little old ladies seeking higher ground hobbled atop their chairs in horror. Several of the braver souls tried to catch the thing; but as soon as they got close, it took off, flapping its wings en route to instill panic in a different section of the room.

"Get it, get it!" people shouted into the bedlam.

"It's over here," someone else screamed.

No one at the head table had the slightest idea what to do, including the board member who had brought the bird to begin with. Half the ladies in the room were laughing, the other half were screaming. Finally one woman yelled into the fray, "Someone get the chef! Get the chef!" For some reason, she must have thought the chef didn't get his chickens all cut and wrapped from Shop Rite, like the rest of us did.

After what seemed like an eternity of pandemonium, one courageous soul made her way into the kitchen and retrieved the cook, who evidently had no fear of live chickens. He captured the poor thing and was advised to put it out of its misery. As for the women, they all had thoroughly enjoyed themselves.

No, I knew my limitations. Public speaking, particularly when accompanied by public humiliation, was not my thing. But Jean was persuasive, and I loved Jean. In those days she managed a Christian bookstore. About twenty years my senior, Jean served on the CWC board, taught Bible, was a key woman in my church, knew just about every Christian in the county, and had a fabulous sense of humor. She was tremendous fun to be around, yet had mastered the delicate art of balance between seriousness and frivolity. She knew when each was appropriate and dispensed them both in perfect dosages accompanied by great and godly wisdom. Although she had spent considerable time in amateur theater before she had become a Christian, not once did I ever know her to flaunt her accomplishments or exhibit a sense of self-importance. On the contrary, Jean valued humility. She sought it for herself and taught me its significance in God's sight. It did not take long before I had "adopted" her as my mother.

As all new believers, I needed someone to teach me the practicalities of biblical living—how to live a life of faith by putting into action what God instructs in the Bible—and how to discern the hand of God and the will of God in your life. At those, Jean was a pro. I would ask questions, and she would open her Bible and show me the answers. She was full of pithy little sayings that were easy to remember, such as, "Believers should never be 'under' the circumstances. We should always be 'above' the circumstances," and "God doesn't want your ability, just your availability." She encouraged me when I was down, praised me when I got something right, tactfully and gently corrected me when I was wrong, and always exhorted me to pray about every-thing, to seek God's face, and to regard the Bible as the only source of truth. "That's how you can spot a lie," she said. "Examine it in light of the Word of God." She was also quick to tell me, "People will fail you. God will never fail you."

At least once a week I found myself in her little office in the bookstore or sitting at her kitchen table nursing a cup of tea while we discussed the things of the Lord. It was in the bookstore where Jean hatched the notion that was to thrust me into public speaking.

"A crayon?" I asked.

"Yes," Jean replied. "A crayon. It's a great idea."

Some great idea. As if it weren't bad enough that I would feel like a moron when I reached the microphone, now I would have to look like one too. "I can't do this," I told her. "It's just not me." Truth be known, it probably wasn't anybody. Who in creation wanted to prance around dressed like a red crayon in a box! Well, maybe I could have found a five-year-old; but I was thirty-one!

"You'll be fine," she said. "I'll paint the box. You just get some red tights, a red shirt, and make a little, pointy red hat out of construction paper. And you write the script."

Swell. Welcome to the world of public humiliation. But I did what I was told. I wrote a script designed to encour-age women to buy the evangelistic Life Publications book-lets, introducing each booklet with a different color that I had somehow incorporated into the sense of the script. Jean got a big old box from somewhere; painted it so expertly that it looked indistinguishable from a real Crayola Crayon box; and I got the red tights, red turtleneck, and made a little red construction-paper hat that would have looked perfectly at home with the word DUNCE emblazoned on it.

"A box?" James looked skeptical when I told him.

"Yeah," I replied, forcing myself to appear upbeat as I explained the scenario to my very dignified and low-keyed husband over dinner one night. "Jean's painted it. It looks exactly like a Crayola Crayon box."

"You're going to wear a box," he repeated, trying his best to digest this unsavory bit of news. Truly, this was not the Lorna he had married. My friends were all church women now, many from my home church but many from churches throughout the county. They had welcomed me into the fold with loving arms, and we shared a strong and unifying spiritual bond. And now I was even willing to make a fool of myself as part of my ministry for the Lord. "Well," James said at last, "if that's what you want to do . . ."

Want may have been too strong a word. When the day of the luncheon arrived, I was so nervous I could not eat. As the time drew near for my grand entrance, I went into the ladies' room to change into my box. The thing was so big a stove could have fit in there with me. Jean had cut holes in the sides for my arms to fit through and a hole in the top for my head. I looked positively ridiculous. Yet I did indeed look like a red crayon.

When I heard my cue, I walked through the crowd, strode onto the platform, went up to the head table, and took my place before the microphone. To my utter amazement, I delivered the announcement with complete ease, explaining the differences between the various booklets and encouraging the women to buy them as gifts for their unsaved family and friends.

That day I learned a valuable lesson. In my weakness, God was strong; and whatever I lacked, He would generously supply so I could serve Him. He was more than able to do all that needed to be done, providing I was willing to be His vessel. That day the Lord privileged me to taste the blessing He bestows upon His children when they lean on Him. He had taken a conservative, timid Jewish woman who avoided public speaking like a disease, dressed her up like a crayon, and stood her before two hundred women to talk about the Lord Jesus. If He could do that, He could do absolutely anything. But then, isn't that what He had already told me? He had said, "with God all things are possible" (Mt. 19:26).

From Life Publications chairman I moved to something else and then to telephone chairman, which taught me the behind-the-scenes, backbone essentials of the CWC ministry. Then I moved into a job that necessitated sitting at the head table and making one announcement each month concerning the missionaries whom the ministry supports. "You do it your own way," Jean told me. "I have a style that suits me. You develop one that suits you." I did—one scrupulously cultivated to avoid self-inflicted mortification. I have never dressed like a big red crayon since!

For a while it seemed as though I was passing through jobs every three or four months. But when the vacancies occurred on the board and someone asked me to fill in, I gladly agreed. In addition to the luncheon, I attended the board meeting each month as well as the monthly prayer coffee. The Lord had given me my niche. He had given me direction, a format in which to serve Him, and wonderful friends. Although I was the only Hebrew Christian in the group, I shared a common situation with many of the other women, particularly those who came from Catholic homes and had few, if any, family members who were Christians.

Often I prayed for people who were not saved, asking God to open their eyes and lead them to Jesus Christ for salvation. I began praying in earnest for several of my neighbors, whom I had grown especially fond of. Many of them were churched (all of them were Gentiles), but none of them had received the new birth. However, I rarely prayed for my own brother's salvation. I tried, but I just could not. I also could not tell him that I had become a Christian.

My brother had married a Presbyterian, something I knew he would not have done had Daddy been alive. We were still in Vermont in those days; and although I was older than he, I had tried hard to act like a sister, not a mother. When I had deduced that he was serious about his college girlfriend, I told him how I felt.

"You need to marry someone Jewish," I had said. "I'm not going to lecture you, and when I'm through I'm never going to mention this again. But I have to tell you how I feel. Religion will always come between you. You need to marry a Jew." My brother took the advice graciously, then did just as he pleased and married her anyway.

I not only followed in his footsteps, but I went one better and asked the Lord Jesus to be my Messiah and to save me from the consequences of my sin. How could I ever explain *that* to him! I did not know and I was afraid to try. A number of years later, however, I learned even more of God's infinite grace and mercy. It turned out that my brother had become a Hebrew Christian four years before I had! While I had been dreading to tell him of my faith in Christ, he and his wife had been praying for me! My sister-in-law had been converted through Campus Crusade for Christ while she and my brother were students at the University of Vermont. She had been instrumental in praying for his salvation.

"As much as I loved him," she told me later, "I never would've married him had he not been saved."

As we all marveled at the great goodness of God, I asked my brother, "If you were already saved, why did you bother to get a rabbi to help perform your wedding ceremony?"

My wonderful brother looked at me, and with a smile on his lips, he replied, "I did that for you."

In March 1983 I was asked to assume the chairmanship of the Executive Board of the Trenton Christian Women's Club. It constituted a substantial commitment of time and energy, and I knew I could only serve in that capacity if my husband agreed. James was happy that I enjoyed the ministry, but he sometimes grew annoyed with the stream of telephone interruptions and the amount of time I devoted to the organization. Just weeks earlier he had told me that the only position he never wanted me to take was the very one I had just been offered.

So the first thing I did was pray. I told the Lord I could not possibly go against my husband, and I asked Him to show me clearly if I was His choice for chairman. "Please Lord," I prayed, "give James a heart that is in total agreement, or I can't take the job."

The next day I spoke to my husband, fully expecting him to tell me "No." I was shocked when he said instead, "I think you should take it."

"Really?" I asked. "I thought you didn't want me to."

"I've changed my mind," James said. "I think you should take it."

So I agreed to become the chairman. Installation of the new Executive Board was scheduled for Wednesday, April 20.

By now Jamie was three and one-half years old. She was a beautiful little girl, with huge gray eyes and a thick mass of curly light brown hair that caused everyone who saw her to fuss over her and remark how much she looked like Shirley Temple. She was enrolled in the nursery school at the Jewish Community Center in Ewing because it had one of the best nursery schools in the state of New Jersey at the time. It was near our home, my teacher friends at church highly recommended it, and James had no objection.

On the Wednesday before the big installation luncheon, Jamie became very sick. She could not stop vomiting. I brought her to the pediatrician, who told me, to my great surprise, that Jamie needed to be hospitalized. Apparently she had contracted both a urinary infection that necessitated she be catheterized and a virus that caused her to vomit, preventing her from taking any medicine by mouth. She needed intravenous feeding.

I could not believe it. How had that happened so quickly? She was fine the day before, and now she needed hospitalization? I did not particularly like hospitals. My husband's stay in Florida still lingered in my mind, as did the painful memory of my mother, who wasted away for four months in a depressing hospital while waiting to die.

"Isn't there another way?" I asked the doctor. She was a good pediatrician. Many of the other doctors in town sent their children to her, and I knew that she had done her residency at Children's Hospital of Philadelphia.

She did not respond. Then I asked, "If Jamie were your daughter, what would you do?"

"I'd bring her to the hospital right away," she replied. So that was that. I checked her into St. Francis Hospital in Trenton, where she was immediately whisked upstairs to pediatrics and taken into a room where I was forbidden to follow.

"We're going to insert a catheter, and you'll hear her scream. We want you to stay outside," I was told.

"Oh Lord," I prayed silently. "Please don't let them hurt my baby." I prayed for her protection, for her healing, for anything I could think of. I had been saved for two years now, had been diligently studying the Word, and I knew that God loved Jamie even more than I did. I had to trust Him to take care of her. It wrenched my heart to hear her screaming and crying behind that closed door, but soon she came out and she was fine. The catheter was in place, as was the intravenous needle that was carrying medicine into her body through a vein in the top of her hand. The nurse told me to keep an eye on the needle. If it slipped, her hand would swell; and in that event, I needed to contact a nurse right away to get it fixed.

I called James. He was shocked and upset. He, too, could not understand how Jamie could become so sick so quickly. By now it was about 3:30 in the afternoon.

"I have the attorneys for the company in my office," he said. "I'll get rid of them and tell them to come back tomorrow morning, and I'll come to the hospital as soon as I can."

I couldn't wait to see him. James was my rock. Steady and calm, he always knew what to do, and I depended on him as I had never depended on anyone else. He arrived around 5 P.M. Jamie was thrilled to see him, showed him all her tubes, and told him she was hungry—a good sign, although she was not allowed to eat for twenty-four hours.

I loved watching the two of them together. Jamie was, in effect, the child of his old age. He was so tender with her, yet he spoke to her as though she were an adult. "She's a smart child," he used to tell me before she could even walk, "and she understands everything you say to her."

I'll never forget the time he decided to take over potty training her because she wasn't coming along fast enough to suit him. His method was unique, if nothing else. Jamie was little more than two years old, but that did not deter my husband from sitting her down on the living room sofa, extolling the virtues of using a bathroom as opposed to a diaper, and then instructing her to use the bathroom. She sat there next to him looking so cute, eyes as big as saucers, her big curls bobbing up and down as she nodded her head in total agreement. "She'll use the bathroom now," he announced with confidence. Needless to say, I kept buying diapers.

Then there was the time he babysat her one afternoon while trying to make repairs in the garage. James had a habit of sticking his tools in the back pocket of his jeans. While he worked in the garage, Jamie waddled around nearby in her diaper.

When it came time to use the screwdriver, it was nowhere to be found. James was meticulous with his tools. He knew he had already used the screwdriver once and remembered exactly where he had placed it.

"I had to use a knife instead," he complained to me afterward. "Do you know how hard it is to unscrew a screw with a knife! And you know where I finally found the screwdriver?"

"No," I said. "Where was it?"

"Jamie had it. She had slid it down the back of her diaper!"

Well, her father put his tools in *his* back pocket, so she figured she would do likewise! I was glad for the time they would be able to share together, even if it was in the hospital. I drove home, packed a bag with things I would need to spend the night there, stuffed my Bible into the bag, and returned to St. Francis Hospital.

When I arrived, James found a nurse to stay in the room with Jamie, and he took me to dinner. He looked so weary. He was fifty-eight years old, and I knew he was tiring of the intense pressure of his job. He talked that night about retiring early, and I knew that he at least needed to go home to North Carolina for a vacation so he could rest.

When we got back to the hospital, Jamie complained again about being hungry.

"Here, honey," her father said, removing a dollar bill from his billfold. "You keep this; and when the doctor says you can eat, you give it to Mama, and she'll go downstairs and buy you anything you want." That brought a smile to her face. He kissed her, told her he would see her tomorrow, and left. I walked him out to the elevator.

"Call me early in the morning," he reminded me, "because I have the attorneys coming back." As we said goodbye, he hesitated, then told me if I needed him to come to the hospital later that night so I could get some sleep, he would be glad to come. "Just call," he said.

I returned to Jamie feeling apprehensive and very depressed. As I looked out her window, I could see my husband walk across the street to his car, turn on the headlights, and drive away. I got out my Bible and began to pray. "Please take care of my husband, Lord. I love him so much. Please bring him home safely. Don't let anything happen to him along the way. Just lay him down in his bed and let him go to sleep."

Around 9 P.M. I decided to call. It calmed me just to hear his mellow, southern voice. "Honey, I just had my hand on the phone to call you," he said. He told me how much he loved me. I told him how much I loved him, and I promised to call early the next morning.

Sleep that night eluded me. After tossing and turning for hours, I finally got up, got out my Bible, read, and prayed. I was worried about James and several times considered driving home to see him. But doing so would leave no one to watch Jamie. Around 3 A.M. I went over to inspect Jamie's hand again, and this time I noticed that it was swollen. Immediately I called the nurse, who verified that the intravenous needle had dislodged and had to be reinserted. Good thing I was right there.

At 6 A.M. I decided to call my husband. He was usually out of the house by 6:45. No one answered, so I assumed he was in the shower. I called again twenty minutes later. Still no answer. What if I had missed him? What if he had already left for the office? There was no hope of reaching him there because the switchboard would be closed for several more hours. I wanted desperately to talk to him. So I found a nurse to stay with Jamie, and I drove home.

James's car was still in the driveway. I pulled in behind it, unlocked the front door, and went upstairs. When I entered our bedroom it was still dark. The drapes were still drawn. My husband was lying in bed, his eyes closed and the covers neatly tucked in. He had seemed so tired the previous day that it occurred to me he might have unplugged the phone, then inadvertently overslept.

"James," I called, as I walked in. "James, it's me."

I walked over to the bed to wake him up, and then I knew. James was dead.

Chapter Five

Ⓢ

Send Someone Else

I will lift up mine eyes unto the hills. From whence
cometh my help? My help cometh from the LORD,
who made heaven and earth (Ps. 121:1–2).

I buried my husband next to his father in the cemetery
across the road from the little white country church
where he grew up, and a part of me will forever rest
with him in the soil of the tobacco fields of North Carolina.
His grave is marked with a double stone on which is
carved one of the many promises of the magnificent
reunion beyond the grave that God has reserved exclusively for those who have been born again:

> *For the Lord himself shall descend from heaven*
> *with a shout, with the voice of the archangel, and*
> *with the trump of God; and the dead in Christ*
> *shall rise first; Then we who are alive and remain*
> *shall be caught up together with them in the*

*clouds, to meet the Lord in the air; and so shall we
ever be with the Lord* (1 Th. 4:16–17).

How I would go on without him I did not know. But
God knew, and it was to Him I clung. I began to depend
on Him for everything, not so much because I wanted to,
but because I had nowhere else to turn.

Because of James's prominence, his death was the lead
story in the newspaper the morning after I found him. It
ran with a photograph and a banner headline across all six
columns of the front page and was carried by the wire services, including the Associated Press and United Press
International, which called me at the hospital. Several days
later the executive editor of the newspaper wrote a beautiful column in James's memory that was read at his funeral
in North Carolina.

I devoured those articles. Over and over again I read
them, staring at James's photograph, trying to grasp the
reality of his death. Although I knew he had suffered a previous heart attack, I never expected the one that finally
killed him. I still visualized him walking up the stairs at
our home or pulling into the driveway after work or talking to Jamie. The last was the hardest.

"I'll see you tomorrow, honey," he had told her. But
tomorrow never came. Jamie remained in the hospital five
days before being discharged, and every day she asked for
her daddy. I could not lie, but neither could I tell her the
truth while she remained in such a strange environment,
connected to all sorts of medical paraphernalia.

"Look at all the people coming to see you," I said, trying
to comfort her by pointing out visitors who had shown up
from everywhere to be with us—my brother and his wife,
in particular, who had flown in from Texas.

"Yes," she said, "but not Daddy."

My answer was always the same. "Daddy can't come, honey. He loves you very much, but he can't come." Finally I was able to bring her home. James's son-in-law, who had immediately flown up from North Carolina when he had heard the news, was with us. As we drove into the driveway, Jamie got excited at seeing her father's car.

"Daddy doesn't know I'm coming home," she announced with delight. I unlocked the front door and she instantly burst out crying. Somehow she knew that something was very wrong. Slowly I eased her onto the living room sofa and explained that her daddy had gone to live in heaven with Jesus, and someday she would see him again.

At first I hesitated to tell her that, because I had been plagued by uncertainty concerning my husband's salvation. Every now and then, James would say something that made me wonder whether he had, indeed, experienced a biblical conversion. Yet he told me he had become a Christian as a teenager; and for the past month, we had been attending a Bible study. He also had been reading his Bible faithfully. So I decided to believe that at some point, —he had truly trusted Jesus as his Savior; and I conveyed that information to my grieving child.

As she sat there on the sofa, just as she had on the day of her daddy's potty-training discourse, she gazed at me with great big gray eyes, and through her tears, she asked plaintively, "What are we going to do with all his clothes? Who's going to light the fireplace?"

At three and one-half years old, my little Jamie had grasped completely the harsh reality of death. Together we sat and cried. How incredibly thankful I was that the Word of God is truth, and that eternal life exists in abundance beyond the grave for everyone who has accepted the redemption offered through the precious blood of Christ. As the apostle Paul wrote, "Eye hath not seen, nor ear heard, neither have entered into the heart of man, the things which God hath prepared for them that love him" (1 Cor. 2:9).

As I spoke with Jamie, I went directly to the throne of God Almighty, the Creator of heaven and earth, who gave me the appropriate words and made good His promise,

> *Peace I leave with you, my peace I give unto you; not as the world giveth, give I unto you. Let not your heart be troubled, neither let it be afraid. . . . In the world ye shall have tribulation: but be of good cheer; I have overcome the world* (Jn. 14:27; 16:33).

Within the hour, the three of us were on a plane for North Carolina. The funeral and burial were scheduled for the day following our arrival. James's son picked us up at the airport in Wilmington. As we made the hour-long trip to the country, my 25-year-old stepson, still somewhat in shock, shook his head as he drove and voiced what all of us were feeling: "I can't believe Daddy is dead," he said. "I just can't believe Daddy is dead."

With that, my little daughter piped up indignantly from the back seat, "My Daddy's not dead. He's alive in heaven." Out of the mouths of babes. . .

Somehow I knew I would feel better once I saw Mrs. Bennett and my sisters-in-law. I praised God every day for them and felt closer to James in their presence, amid the dogwoods, azaleas, and crepe myrtle trees beneath the blue skies of the North Carolina that my husband had loved so much.

I stayed there as long as I could. Eventually, though, I had to face returning to New Jersey. When I arrived home, everything seemed strangely unreal. I missed James so much that my chest ached continually, and within the space of three weeks, I had lost almost thirty pounds. I could not think of James without feeling physical pain; yet he was all I *could* think about.

The day I returned home, I walked around the bedroom noting things that made it seem as though he would be right back, such as the change he had left on the dresser when he had emptied his pockets before going to bed. It was a week before I gathered it up and put it away. Sliding open his closet door, I grabbed hold of the sleeve of one of his suits, fell down on the floor, and cried.

For six months I hardly slept. Some nights I talked to the Lord for hours, then dozed off and woke up an hour later to talk to Him again or read my Bible. My heart broke for my little girl, who would never really know her father. How would she fare without him? How would she handle *her* loss? How would I ever be able to explain what a wonderful father she had had? How was I going to rear her all alone? Yet in my despair, God always assured me that I was never alone, nor would I ever be again. I ingested verses such as,

> *Fear thou not; for I am with thee. Be not dismayed; for I am thy God. I will strengthen thee; yea, I will help thee; yea, I will uphold thee with the right hand of my righteousness* (Isa. 41:10).

> *When thou passest through the waters, I will be with thee; and through the rivers, they shall not overflow thee; when thou walkest through the fire, thou shalt not be burned, neither shall the flame kindle upon thee* (Isa. 43:2).

He promised me, "I will never leave thee, nor forsake thee" (Heb. 13:5); and He always extended His invitation to "come boldly unto the throne of grace" to find mercy and help in time of need (Heb. 4:16). I memorized those verses and hung onto them for dear life. It seemed that when I needed help the most, the Word of God would pop into my head and provide relief.

The pain did not diminish much as the months went by. For a while it actually grew worse, though I managed to keep my misery well hidden from all but my closest friends. I hung pictures of James everywhere because I wanted so desperately to see his face.

About six months after his death, I became sick. It was nothing serious, but it was sufficient to initiate me into the tribulations of single-parenthood. How was I ever going to care for Jamie? I could hardly think straight. Just as I was complaining to God, my friend Marie called. Marie was the only woman in my neighborhood who still had young children at home, and it did not take her long to realize I was in no condition to care for an active 4 year-old.

"Let me come up and get Jamie," she said. "I'll bring her to my house to play, then I'll bring her back." I was so grateful. She was a wonderful friend to me. After she collected Jamie, I got back in bed, reached for my Bible, and began to read. But reading did not help. Soon I could not even remember what I had read or what book of the Bible was even open. Sitting there feeling ill, surrounded by a gallery of photographs of my husband and missing him terribly, I sank into a pit of misery and depression so deep that I lacked the desire to even climb out.

Certainly God made no mistakes. His plan was perfect and all His ways just. Yet repeating that fact in my head did not remove the agony in my heart. And the more I longed for my husband, the deeper I sank in self-pity and the angrier I became with God.

Finally I could take it no longer. "Lord," I yelled, "do you really know what I'm going through? Do you really understand?" The more miserable I felt, the louder I shouted.

"Do you really know how much I miss him!" I screamed at the top of my lungs. As the tears slid down my cheeks, I looked up at the ceiling and shrieked in bitterness, "Do you even understand? Are you even up there? Can you even hear me!"

"What's the use," I thought. Hysteria was not going to do me any good. I had to keep reading my Bible. But where was I reading? I had no idea. And I didn't even care.

But clearly, God was my only hope. So I tried to regain my composure. I wiped my eyes and forced myself to begin again. As I glanced down at my Bible, the most amazing words stared up at me: "I love the LORD, because he hath heard my voice and my supplications. Because he hath inclined his ear unto me, therefore will I call upon him as long as I live" (Ps. 116:1–2).

God was speaking to *me*. His "voice" was indisputably clear and His words as warm and soothing as afternoon sunlight. I felt compelled to continue reading.

> *The sorrows of death compassed me, and the pains of sheol got hold upon me; I found trouble and sorrow. Then called I upon the name of the LORD: O LORD, I beseech thee, deliver my soul. Gracious is the LORD, and righteous; yea, our God is merciful* (Ps. 116: 3–5).

How unbelievable was my God. He indeed was "up there." He indeed had heard me, and He was bearing me up in His everlasting arms. Every word of Scripture comforted my soul. Still, I felt God had more to communicate, so I continued reading. Then I reached verse 15. "Precious in the sight of the LORD is the death of his saints."

That day the God of Israel reached down into my pit and lifted me out. He set my feet upon a rock and showed me yet again His endless and personal love for me. In my sojourn through this valley of heartache and pain, the Lord Jesus brought me one step closer to Himself, by faith.

How many times had I heard it said, "God helps those who help themselves." What a lie! God helps those who are incapable of helping themselves. God helps the weak and the humble and the powerless, and He resists the proud and the arrogant. God was not wanting me to be strong or to "tough it out." He wanted me to learn that, in my weakness, He was strong and that I could lean entirely on Him. He wanted me to learn what He had taught King David: "Taste and see that the LORD is good; blessed is the man who trusteth in him" (Ps. 34:8). As David, the sweetest psalmist in Israel, wrote, "This poor man cried, and the LORD heard him, and saved him out of all his troubles" (Ps. 34:6).

Losing James was the single event I had dreaded most in life. Many a night I had lain in bed next to him, praying for him, thanking the Lord for the wonderful husband He had given me, and begging God, "Please Lord, you can take everything—the house, the money, the fancy car—You can have it all. But please, oh please, just don't take my husband."

To that request God had answered "No." In His infinite wisdom, He had decided to take my husband and to show me anew how much He loved me. Through my trouble, the Lord enabled me to taste firsthand the genuineness of His promise, "The LORD is near unto all those who call upon him, to all who call upon him in truth" (Ps.145:18) and to experience the peace that comes from "Casting all your care upon him; for he careth for you" (1 Pet. 5:7).

He was the One who loved me better than anyone else possibly could, including my beloved James. And He was the One who was able to keep me, to protect me, and to give me His strength for the days to come. Truly, God had given me exceedingly great and precious promises, and He was teaching me that He would faithfully keep every single one of them. Never again did I sink so low. That day God began, as the prophet Joel wrote, to restore "the years that the locust hath eaten" (Joel 2:25).

During the next two years, I spent a lot of time with my mother-in-law in North Carolina. I continued as chairman of Christian Women's Club—a blessing of incalculable proportion—and Jamie finished nursery school and embarked on kindergarten.

I began working part-time, and somewhere along the way, bit by imperceptible bit, the inevitable happened. Life returned to normal. I still missed James, but the wrenching pain in my chest finally disappeared. The anguish of remembering gradually subsided, and the thoughts of my husband and our life together at last began to blossom into fragrant memories.

By the spring of 1985 I was standing at a crossroads. At thirty-five years old, I began to wonder what on earth I was going to do with the rest of my life.

I hate snow. Sacrilegious though it may sound coming from a native Vermonter, it nevertheless is the unexaggerated truth. Growing up, of course, I felt differently. I actually loved the stuff, particularly when it packed down nicely to form a smooth runway for my Flexible Flyer, which I grudgingly shared with my brother. But, having never learned to ski, by the time I had become a reporter, the delights of winter had melted conclusively into one monumental aggravation.

Consequently, when the Lord made it clear He wanted me to move to Schroon Lake, New York, where children hoisted their sleds onto the school bus every day and snow had been known to entirely entomb automobiles until spring, I had mixed emotions. If only Word of Life Bible Institute were in Bermuda! Now there was a place I would have gone with pleasure. But Schroon Lake was located a stone's throw from Vermont in freeze-your-nose-off, thermal underwear territory. "Only for You, Lord," I said. "I wouldn't do this for anyone but You."

God had planted the Bible institute high, high, high in the Adirondacks, as Jack Wyrtzen used to say on his radio broadcasts; and that was exactly where the Lord now wanted to plant me. I had only been a Hebrew Christian for four and one-half years, and I did not know much about Word of Life or Jack Wyrtzen, the man whom God had used to raise up this massive organization that spanned six continents and reached thousands of people each year with the good news of salvation through faith in Jesus, the Messiah of Israel.

I did know, however, that in those days, Word of Life's only Bible Institute in North America was in Schroon Lake, and that was where I had to go. My friend Marilyn suggested I contact George and Marcia Slothower. For years the Slothowers had been leaders in our church before they pulled up stakes and relocated to Schroon Lake to serve the Lord in full-time work through Word of Life, whose worldwide headquarters was also there.

Since George and Marcia had moved shortly after James and I began attending church, I never really knew them and felt awkward asking total strangers for help. But Marilyn assured me that they would gladly welcome both

Jamie and me and help us find a place to live. So I called. Unbeknown to me, so had Marilyn.

"I was expecting to hear from you," Marcia said cheerfully. "We'd be thrilled to have you come stay with us, and I'll take you around to the various places that are for rent. I know we'll find something."

I don't know what proved to be the greater blessing that summer, finding a place to live or finding George and Marcia. To me, they were the quintessential Christians—sincere, friendly, loving, hospitable and kind, with never a mean or negative word about anything. Their lives reflected the daily joy of walking with the Lord Jesus, and nothing ever seemed to irritate them into complaining. I enjoyed being around them immensely, valued their sound counsel, and treasured their influence on Jamie.

On the day after our arrival, we set out house hunting. Now, Schroon Lake in the summer bore no resemblance to Schroon Lake in the winter. In the summer the weather was warm, the sun inviting, the flowers plentiful and bursting with color, and the stores and restaurants—all located within the same block in the heart of town—were bustling with people. Because of summer residents and vacationers, the combination gas station/mini-mart/ice cream shop usually served a steady stream of customers who milled around outside near picnic tables, and the traffic occasionally backed up on Route 9 (the only road through Schroon Lake). To the untrained eye, this picturesque hamlet, with its sandy little public beach right in the heart of town, seemed a delightfully easy place to live.

Then came winter. Goodbye flowers, hello snowbanks. Gone was the modest hubbub in town because shop owners and restauranteurs had, for the most part, fled south.

The sidewalks rolled up, as they say, around 5 P.M., unless, of course, it snowed. Then they rolled up earlier—not that anyone could actually *see* a sidewalk between November and April. With the summer cottages locked up tight for winter, traffic virtually disappeared from Route 9, and the only place to buy groceries for miles around in those days was one store with a leaky roof in the heart of the village. When I was there, the town had one pharmacist whose drugstore also occupied a spot on the business block, as did the only laundromat, the post office, and the bank.

Winter made life hard in the Adirondacks. For starters, either you shoveled snow or you paid someone else to do it. You routinely carried a shovel and a bag of gravel or sand in the trunk of your car in case you got stuck somewhere and needed to dig yourself out; you always kept candles around in case the power went out; you kept battery-operated radios and flashlights in good working order, with lots of spare batteries; and so on and so forth. Many year-round residents also burned wood, either as a primary or alternative source of heat.

Some said the harshness of the weather was why people there were so extremely nice. They helped each other out and offset the severities of winter by sincerely caring for one another.

I was not thinking about any of those things when Marcia took me to find a rental. For weeks I had been asking the Lord to pick out the perfect home for Jamie and me and to lead us directly to it. With the flowers in bloom and the sun shining, I never gave a thought to winter and just concentrated on finding a nice place to live. Not until later did I realized how carefully and completely God had looked out for me.

The first place we investigated was a little red cottage in the center of town located spitting distance from the grocery store and a few yards from the property owners' house across the driveway. They, too, were Word of Lifers; and I instantly liked the wife, who showed us the place. But the cottage was very small, with only one bedroom and a sofa bed in the living room. I couldn't see being so cramped.

So we moved to the next available rental. It was much larger and located several miles outside town, in a much more isolated setting. There was little around it, not even houses. Then came the next place. It was lovely but way too expensive. The place after that was way too large. On and on it went, until I finally looked at Marcia, she looked at me, and we said almost in unison, "The first place was the one."

So I rented the little red cottage from Rick and Annie Grahame, and it wasn't until I started school at the end of September that God showed me how, in my utter ignorance, He had provided for my every need. It turned out that I had to leave for school thirty minutes before Jamie, who was entering first grade.

"No problem," said Rick. "Send her over here. She'll stay with my kids, then they'll all walk to the bus together." And that was exactly what they did every single day of that entire school year. How I praised God that the Grahame children and Jamie all attended the local Christian school; that the bus stop was only one block away; that I had off-street parking; that Rick always shoveled the walkways and emptied the mouse traps (yuck!); and that the grocery store, the bank, the post office, and the laundromat were all within easy walking-distance of my cozy little home. But most of all, I thanked the Lord for Rick and Annie, who were never more than a few footsteps away.

In placing me with the Grahames, the Lord had not only provided abundantly for my material needs—all of which had most definitely eluded me—but He had cared for my emotional needs as well. Rick's and Annie's friendship became dear to me and played a considerable role in keeping me from feeling isolated and alone.

No wonder the Lord Jesus admonished His disciples not to worry about anything, because their Heavenly Father already knew everything they needed and would provide (Mt. 6:25-34). The Lord knew what I needed better than I did, and He provided generously.

He even provided an atmosphere devoid of distractions so I could study. In fact, I was so free of distractions I couldn't find any if I tried. The mountains prevented my radio from picking up anything intelligible; and without cable, the snow on my television was so bad I finally gave the set away. Consequently, I went to bed each night at 8:30 and got a much-needed eight and one-half hours of sleep before having to get up at 5 A.M.

God had made Himself clear. He wanted me to concentrate on studying, something I had not done in about fifteen years. Unlike the vast majority of the other four hundred students, I had not come to the Bible Institute out of high school. Fortunately, we had approximately fifteen married couples, among whom I was numbered. Most of us had given up careers, sold or rented our homes, and generally sacrificed in other tangible ways to be able to devote an entire year to studying the Word of God. And study we did. Though the workload was not difficult, it was voluminous; and once you fell behind, you had to run twice as fast to catch up.

That year I was probably more organized than I have ever been in my life. Organization, to my mind, was the key to survival. Classes ended around lunchtime each day, so I studied all afternoon before Jamie came home from school and again after she went to bed. I never worked on weekends because I devoted that time to her.

The married students all carpooled to the campus. They graciously exempted me from driving, but never failed to pick me up every morning and bring me home after class. Usually we would arrive at Council Hall before the students who lived on campus. It worked out well because it gave us a chance to chat.

One day in early October, someone introduced me to a married student named Bruce. "She's Jewish," my friend had said. Somehow that fact escaped no one and excited everyone, just as it had at my church. For the first time in my life, I was meeting people who actually wished they had been born Jewish. How unbelievable! These Gentiles, all of whom were born again, had all placed their faith in the Jewish Messiah. They knew the magnificent prophecies God had yet to fulfill concerning Israel, and they had a love for God's Chosen People.

Bruce peered at me seriously, then asked almost accusingly, "Are you burdened for your people?"

I was almost afraid to tell him the truth. I knew what he was implying. He may just as well have asked, "Are you going to carry the gospel to the Jewish people?" Well, the answer to that was no, no, and no again.

It wasn't that I didn't want them to know the truth. I just knew how hard it would be for them to accept it. For the most part, my people despised the very name of Jesus, and I knew and understood why. Telling them that "there is no other name under heaven given among men, whereby we must be saved" (Acts 4:12), took infinitely more courage than I possessed. It had taken me two years just to marshal enough courage to tell my own brother that I had placed my faith in Jesus. I knew how most Jewish people would feel about me. I could almost hear them screaming, "You're not fit to call yourself a Jew!"

"Let someone else go to my people, Bruce," I said. "It would be too difficult for me. Let God send someone else."

Send someone else. That had become my credo after the little taste of witnessing I had received one day while dropping Jamie off at nursery school at the Jewish Community Center. I was just about to drive away when a little, elderly Jewish lady rapped on my car door. I rolled down the window.

"Yes?"

"Can you give me a ride home?" she inquired with an extremely thick European accent. I had never seen her before.

"Where do you live?" I asked.

"In Trenton." Rarely did I drive into Trenton; and when I did, I always got lost. Wanting to help her though, I opened the car door and welcomed her inside. She gave me directions and we drove off. Before I could even initiate a conversation, she looked at me and demanded to know, "Are you Jewish?"

"Yes," I replied. Then I hastened to add, "But I believe Jesus is the Messiah." You would have thought I had just told her I had typhoid. Her face froze. She pressed her slight frame up against the car door, clutched her handbag, and had she been able, I think she would have hurled her little body out into the street just to get away from me. She said nothing. She just stared ahead.

So I plunged along, undaunted. I gave her more Bible verses to substantiate my beliefs than anyone could have assimilated in a year. As we neared her apartment building, I stopped, grabbed a pen and paper, and jotted down some Scriptures for her to read, including Isaiah 53, Jeremiah 31, and Micah 5:2.

The woman took the paper without a word. Then she opened the car door and stepped outside. "How many children do you have?" she asked, leaning in over the seat she had just vacated.

"Just one," I said.

In a voice brimming with anger and contempt, she thrust a bony finger in my face and shouted, "It's a good thing you have only one child to ruin!" With that, she slammed the car door and stalked off.

No, telling Jewish people about Jesus was not for me. I had already talked to the Lord about it. We had an understanding. "I'll go anywhere you want Lord. I just can't go to the Jewish people. They're too hostile to Jesus and too tough to reach." How well I knew. Seven years earlier, when I was sewing my maternity top, that hostile, tough-to-reach Jewish lady had been me.

Let God send someone else. Evidently that answer did not satisfy Bruce. "You need to be burdened for your people," he said, wagging his finger two inches from my nose. "And I'm going to pray every day that God gives you a burden for your people."

Fine. But as far I was concerned, the matter was settled.

The sovereignty of God versus the free will of man. That was one of the heady, theological topics covered in class on

October 25, 1985. It fascinated me enough that when I returned to my little cottage to study that afternoon, I decided to give humanity the benefit of my vast repository of theological wisdom and knowledge and solve the antinomy that has baffled the world's wisest and most learned Bible scholars for centuries. First I made myself comfortable at the kitchen table and poured myself a nice hot cup of coffee—an essential prerequisite to deep thinking.

Then I opened my Bible and began what I believed would be my excursion into the realm of the great thinkers. Of course, I had not a clue where to begin. Inexplicably, I found myself in the book of Romans—chapter 11, verse 1: "I say, then," wrote the apostle Paul, "Hath God cast away his people? God forbid. For I also am an Israelite, of the seed of Abraham, of the tribe of Benjamin."

Well, I thought, this was an interesting place to begin, with the Jewishness of the apostle Paul.

> God hath not cast away his people whom he foreknew. Know ye not what the scripture saith of Elijah? how he maketh intercession to God against Israel, saying, Lord, they have killed thy prophets, and dug down thine altars; and I am left alone, and they seek my life. But what saith the answer of God unto him? I have reserved to myself seven thousand men who have not bowed the knee to the image of Baal. Even so, then, at this present time also there is a remnant according to the election of grace (vv. 2–4).

Indeed, Jewish history is a study of remnants. Though the nation as a whole rarely followed God, the Lord always reserved for Himself a remnant who trusted in Him—men such as Moses, Joshua, Caleb, David, Elijah, Josiah, Daniel. Israel went into captivity in Babylon and returned to the

land with only a remnant under the leadership of
Zerubbabel.   When Nehemiah rebuilt the walls of
Jerusalem, he did so with a remnant. When Ezra restored
true worship, he did so with a remnant.

By the time the Lord Jesus had arrived on the scene, only
a remnant was even looking for Messiah despite the fact
that God had specified in the Hebrew Scriptures exactly
when Messiah would be present on the earth. In Daniel
9:25–26, God said specifically,

> *Know, therefore, and understand, that from the
> going forth of the commandment to restore and to
> build Jerusalem unto the Messiah, the Prince,
> shall be seven weeks, and threescore and two
> weeks; the street shall be built again, and the wall,
> even in troublous times. And after threescore and
> two weeks shall Messiah be cut off, but not for
> himself; and the people of the prince that shall
> come shall destroy the city and the sanctuary, and
> the end of it shall be with a flood, and unto the end
> of the war desolations are determined.*

Here was an incredible prophecy. It so keenly pinpointed
the time of Messiah's appearance that it astounded me when
I had first read it. In the Old Testament, some *weeks* are composed of seven days each and others of seven years each
(Lev. 25:3–4, 8–10). Here the context indicated weeks of
years. Consequently, each *week* actually denoted a period of
seven years. Thus, from the decree to restore and rebuild
Jerusalem until Messiah the Prince, there would be *seven
weeks* (49 years) plus *threescore and two weeks*, (434 years), for
a grand total of 69 weeks, or 483 years as calculated using
prophetic years of 360 days each.

The decree to rebuild Jerusalem was issued in 445 B.C.
Based on the prophecy, the 69 weeks had to end in A.D. 32,

after which Messiah was to be "cut off" and Jerusalem and the Temple destroyed.

Of course, when Daniel received this insight, there was not even a Temple to destroy. Both the city and the sanctuary were still lying in ashes from the time Nebuchadnezzar had destroyed them in 586 B.C., making these Scriptures all the more remarkable.

With one swift stroke, God had revealed to Daniel that Daniel's beloved city would be rebuilt, that a second Temple would someday stand, that Messiah would come, that Messiah would be killed, and that the city and Temple would be destroyed all over again.

There was but one person in all of history who was present on the earth in A.D. 32 who claimed to be Messiah (Mk. 14:61–62; Lk. 23:3; Jn. 4:26, Jn. 5:39–47), who claimed to be God (Jn. 5:18, 8:58, 10:30–33), who had the legal right to sit on the throne of David (Mt. 1:1-17, Lk. 3:23–38), and who was "cut off but not for himself" (Isa. 53) prior to the Roman destruction of Jerusalem and the second Temple in A.D. 70. That person was Yeshua.

In fact, at the end of the first sixty-nine weeks in A.D. 32, the Lord Jesus actually entered the city of Jerusalem riding on a donkey to shouts of "Hosanna," (Jn. 12:12–15) in fulfillment of the Hebrew Scriptures that read,

> *Rejoice greatly, O daughter of Zion; shout, O daughter of Jerusalem; behold, thy King cometh unto thee; he is just, and having salvation; lowly, and riding upon an ass, and upon a colt, the foal of an ass* (Zech. 9:9).

As I sat there reading, I could not help but contemplate the precision of the information God had given us in the Hebrew Scriptures so we could identify our Messiah. He had, in fact, answered all the questions any good reporter would ask: who, what, when, where, and why.

Who was the Messiah to be?

* He was to be God Himself: Isaiah 9:6–7; Isaiah 44:6; Micah 5:2.
* He was to be a direct descendant of and heir to the throne of King David: 1 Chronicles 17:11–14; Isaiah 9:7; 11:1, 10; Jeremiah 33:15–17; Psalm 89:3–4.

What would the Messiah do?

* He would bear our sins and die as a sacrificial lamb: Isaiah 53.
* He would arise from the dead: Psalm 16:10; Isaiah 53:10; Zechariah 12:10.
* He would be a light to the Gentiles: Isaiah 11:10; 49:6.
* He will return to earth a second time to save Israel from destruction: Zechariah 12:8–10; 14:3–5.
* He will reign on the throne of David with righteousness and justice over a Kingdom that will have no end: Isaiah 9:7; 11; Daniel 2:44.

When would the Messiah be here?

* He would be here in A.D. 32 and would die prior to the destruction of the city of Jerusalem and the second Temple in A.D. 70: Daniel 9:25–26.

Where would the Messiah come from?

* He would be born in Bethlehem: Micah 5:2.
* He would minister and live in Galilee of the Gentiles: Isaiah 9:1–2.

Why do we need a Messiah?

* He is the only one who can pay our sin debt: Isaiah 53.

How much plainer could anything be? The facts were all there. Yet only a remnant believed. Why? The Lord Jesus Himself answered that question: "For had ye believed Moses, ye would have believed me" (Jn. 5:46). In the final

analysis, it all boiled down to lack of faith. As the prophet
Daniel said, "O Lord, to us belongeth confusion of face, to
our kings, to our princes, and to our fathers, because we
have sinned against thee" (Dan. 9:8).

But why was I thinking about such things now? Why
was I even in Romans chapter 11? My intent was not to
dwell on the spiritual condition of the Jewish people, but
rather to ponder the great theological mystery of God's
sovereignty versus man's free will. I continued reading.
Using the analogy of an olive tree, Paul addressed the
Gentiles, warning them against feeling superior to the
Jews. The Jews, he said, are the natural branches, and the
Gentiles are but the wild branches. The Gentiles who
believe the truth are grafted into the Jewish root—the
Abrahamic covenant of blessing—from which the Jews are
broken off due to unbelief.

Then I read verse 23: "And they also, if they abide not
still in unbelief, shall be grafted in; for God is able to graft
them in again."

Who could mistake the unparalleled, steadfast love
God has for the Jewish people? During the days of Isaiah,
He promised he would never forsake them and would
always love them better than a nursing mother loves her
own child—even as He was pronouncing judgment
against them.

> Can a woman forget her nursing child, that she
> should not have compassion on the son of her
> womb? Yea, they may forget, yet will I not forget
> thee. Behold, I have engraved thee upon the palms
> of my hands; thy walls are continually before me
> (Isa. 49:15–16).

When the Jewish people rejected the Lord Jesus, He
lamented over them:

O Jerusalem, Jerusalem, thou that killest the prophets, and stonest them who are sent unto thee, how often would I have gathered thy children together, even as a hen gathereth her chickens under her wings, and ye would not! (Mt. 23:37).

Today, as a nation, we have been set aside for a time because, in our present state, God cannot use us to bring spiritual truth to the world. But someday, the Jewish people will repent, and as the prophet Zechariah wrote, "they shall look upon me whom they have pierced, and they shall mourn for him, as one mourneth for his only son" (Zech 12:10).

Then God will restore to us the Kingdom of David, and "in those days," the Bible says, "it shall come to pass that ten men shall take hold out of all languages of the nations, even shall take hold of the skirt of him that is a Jew, saying, We will go with you; for we have heard that God is with you" (Zech. 8:23).

Now, as Gentiles teach the truth of everlasting life through the Messiah of Israel, God stands ready to graft individual Jewish people back into their own root—just as He had grafted me. For in His perfect and divine sovereignty, God is, indeed, "able to graft them in again."

That afternoon, for the first time since I had been saved, I wept bitterly for my people, who are lost without Christ. How many more would go to their graves without ever having heard or having received an invitation to accept the good news that the final sacrifice for their sin has been made? All they have to do now is believe and receive Messiah's gift of forgiveness and everlasting life; "and him that cometh to me," says the Lord Jesus, "I will in no wise cast out" (Jn. 6:37). "For whosoever shall call upon the name of the Lord shall be saved" (Rom. 10:13).

The words of Romans 10:14–15 came quickly to mind.

How, then, shall they call on him in whom they have not believed? And how shall they believe in him of whom they have not heard? And how shall they hear without a preacher? And how shall they preach, except they be sent?

As I sat there at my kitchen table, weeping and asking forgiveness for having been too cowardly and too unwilling to go to the Jewish people, the Lord settled the issue once and for all. I did not see a vision. The heavens did not open. No choir of angels appeared singing hallelujahs. Nor did I hear an audible voice. But God projected His words into my mind as distinctly and unmistakably as if He had bent down and whispered them into my ear. "Lorna," He said, "I am calling you to Israel."

I could not begin to know then how God would fulfill His call. But I understood that whatever direction my life took from then on would involve sharing the liberating news of eternal redemption through Messiah Jesus with my own people. Funny, but I knew one more thing too. I would never be happy doing anything else.

A few days later I saw Bruce. "You can stop praying," I told him. "Your prayers have been answered."

Chapter Six

Jack and Joan

I don't remember exactly how I met Jack Wyrtzen. I do remember he was seventy-three at the time and had been a widower since his wife Marge went home to be with the Lord on New Year's Day, 1984—eight months after James's death. Despite his age, it did not take me long to realize that compared to him, I felt like an old woman. Never had I seen a man with so much white hair have so much energy. He was tireless and could exhaust people less than half his age. His youthful enthusiasm and vitality were legendary, but not as legendary as his faith.

God had converted Jack when he was nineteen years old. He was working in the insurance business and directing his own dance band when the Most High God grabbed hold of him, changed his direction forever, and began to use him in a way that touched the lives of millions of people for God around the world. After he became a Christian in the early 1930s, he began preaching on street corners in

New York City during his lunch hour. Soon he and a small group of fellow believers began holding meetings, winning people to the Lord. Then, in 1941, the rally and radio ministry was born. The rallies became so big that thousands flocked to places such as Madison Square Garden, Carnegie Hall, and even Yankee Stadium to hear Jack preach, with thousands more overflowing into the streets of Manhattan.

For fifty years Jack's worldwide radio broadcasts proclaimed God's life-changing message of forgiveness and eternal life through Jesus Christ. Over the years Word of Life acquired five hundred acres of property in Schroon Lake, New York, which now house an elegant conference center, a host of Bible camps for young people, the organization's international headquarters, and the Bible Institute.

Today Word of Life spans the globe, reaching both metropolitan cities and isolated rural areas with the Word of God. Word of Life church clubs and Bible camps and Bible institutes are everywhere. And anywhere you go, you can find people who received new life in Christ through the ministry of Word of Life or Jack Wyrtzen.

As far as Jack was concerned, no work was more important than carrying the message of hope and salvation through the Jewish Messiah to a lost and dying world. For more than sixty years, he faithfully proclaimed that message and lived his life according to the standards and practices set forth in the Word of God. You had to trust the Lord enough, he believed, to do God's work God's way if you expected to reap God's blessing. He often said, "You can't do the will of God if you don't know the Word of God," and he placed the highest priority on regular Bible study and having a daily quiet time with the Lord. Truly, he was one of the twentieth century's giants of the Christian faith. Books have been written about him and many more, no doubt, will be.

Although I cannot remember how we met, I do remember someone standing up in Council Hall at the end of classes one winter morning and making the following announcement: "Will the Jewish woman who used to be a newspaper reporter please report to the Inn to do the radio broadcast with Jack Wyrtzen."

The Inn was Word of Life's big conference center for adults, and it was where Jack taped his famous radio messages. "Oh no," I moaned. I still disliked public speaking, and the instant I heard the announcement, a giant knot formed in the pit of my stomach. I became so nervous that the expectation of lunch in ten minutes now made me feel sick. What in the world did he want me to say? All I could envision was stammering like a fool for the entire world to hear. True, I would not be decked out like a red crayon; but now I was beginning to wonder if that would be preferable.

Fortunately, I managed to escape. I had an important ministry that day which interfered, and the ministry came first. Everyone understood, especially Jack Wyrtzen. Several months later, the same announcement was made and I escaped yet again for the same reason. By now I was relatively confident that the jaws of radio would never clamp hold of me.

In early spring, I ran into Jack during Wednesday night prayer meeting in church. Although he often couldn't remember my name, he always remembered my face and the pertinent facts: I was Jewish, I was a widow, I had a daughter, and I had been a newspaper reporter.

"I want to get you on the radio some time," he said, speaking briskly. "And I want you to meet Joan," he added, as he began fishing around in his wallet for a picture of her he could show me. "As soon as she moves up here, I want you to have dinner with us. And you can bring that little girl of yours."

By now I knew, as did everyone else at Word of Life, that Jack was engaged to be married in May to a recently widowed business executive from Kansas. For some reason, he felt it was important I get to know her.

I had no objections; but that night I had more pressing things on my mind. School was drawing to a close. Classes would end in mid-May, after which Jamie and I were scheduled to move onto Word of Life Island, where I would work through August. After that, well, only God knew what I would do; and He was keeping that information entirely to Himself.

What I needed, I concluded, was sound, godly counsel. So I began to pray earnestly that God would lead me to two people whom He would use to guide me in the direction He wanted me to go. Those people turned out to be my pastor in Schroon Lake (a man Marcia Slothower held in highest regard) and Dr. Charles Scheide, who was guest lecturer at the Bible Institute. I knew of Dr. Scheide before I ever moved to New York because, in those days, he pastored a large church back home in New Jersey. I was aware that he had rejected an offer to become a candidate for pastor at my home church in Ewing. He had an excellent reputation, and his teaching at the Bible Institute was insightful, practical, and down-to-earth—just what I was looking for.

First came the meeting with my pastor one afternoon in his study. Although I knew the Lord had called me to teach my own people, I never broadcasted that fact. Besides, I was hard-pressed to figure out just how or when I was supposed to get started. Maybe I needed more education? Education is always good. Dallas Theological Seminary, perhaps? I threw that suggestion out and my pastor stomped on it in a hurry.

"What you need," said Dr. Roger Ellison, "is The Friends of Israel Gospel Ministry."

"What exactly is that?" I asked.

Dr. Ellison explained that The Friends of Israel was a sound, effective, worldwide Bible-teaching organization headquartered in New Jersey. It had a growing publishing ministry, he said, into which I probably would fit like a hand in a glove.

"Really?" I asked. "You don't think I might need more education?"

"Lorna," he replied, "in your situation, I think more education would be the last thing on earth you need. Remember when God called Moses at the burning bush, and Moses didn't feel up to the task of confronting Pharaoh or persuading the Israelites to follow him?"

"Yes," I said, wondering where he was going with this line of questioning.

"What did God ask Moses? He asked him 'What is that in your hand?' What was in Moses' hand?"

"A rod," I said.

"Exactly. Something he probably had used almost every day for forty years. What is in your hand, Lorna?"

"I'm a writer and editor," I said.

"That's right," my pastor replied. "And what makes you think that God won't use what He has already put in your hand?"

I had not written anything in years. In fact, I was not even sure I could do it anymore. "If only God would let me write again," I thought, "what an unbelievable blessing that would be." The Friends of Israel. Well, at least it was something to think about.

"So," said Dr. Scheide, "What can I do for you?" The student lounge was not crowded, and we managed to find comfortable seats where we could talk in relative quiet. I explained my background and my situation, told Pastor Scheide I had been praying about talking to him, and asked his advice.

Within minutes Dr. Scheide declared, "What you need is The Friends of Israel Gospel Ministry."

I began to laugh. "That's exactly what my pastor said!"

"It's perfect for you," he said. "It's a fantastic ministry. It publishes an outstanding magazine, *Israel My Glory*, as well as many other good materials. It's extremely sensitive to Jewish people and could probably use your skills. You know what?" he said congenially, "I'm going to write to them and tell them they need you." And that was exactly what he did.

Several weeks later I received a letter from The Friends of Israel encouraging me to arrange an interview. In May, when classes ended, I prepared to trade my little space in Schroon Lake for an even bitsier space—one room in a three-room, motel-like structure affectionately dubbed Little Wheels on Word of Life Island. It was then I took the time to drive down to New Jersey and interview with The Friends of Israel. But if I had thought the trip would settle things, I could not have been more wrong.

The Friends of Israel made no commitment to me. So I explained that if FOI did not need me in September, I would probably enroll in Child Evangelism Fellowship's teacher-training institute in Missouri. I had worked with CEF all year teaching children in the Schroon Lake area and had enjoyed it. CEF's methods and materials were top notch, the course was only four months long, the training would come in handy, and the arrangements would at least provide a place for me to live when I had to vacate the Island. That way, if The Friends of Israel wanted me in January, I would still be available. I said my goodbyes and left the interview knowing no more about my future than when I had arrived—and not knowing was about to kill me.

It's amazing how, in our sojourn through life, the Lord appears to lead us down little side trails to teach us a specific lesson. But in the end, the side trails turn out to have been the major highways, and the lesson turns out to have been the same lesson, over and over and over again. Hundreds of times I had heard, "Trust in the LORD with all thine heart, and lean not unto thine own understanding. In all thy ways acknowledge him, and he shall direct thy paths" (Prov. 3:5–6). "Wait, I say, on the LORD" (Ps. 27:14). So what did I do? After much prayer, I did the complete opposite.

I enrolled my daughter in school in Missouri and secured housing in the CEF dormitory. I had the time. I had the money. I had nothing else to do. Since my home in New Jersey was rented, I had no place to live after graduation on August 24, and this neat little arrangement seemed to solve that problem for four months, anyway. It was workable. It was logical. No one could say it was not worthwhile, and it offered me a temporary feeling of security. Never mind, of course, that it had not one thing in the world to do with the fact that God wanted me to go back to my own people.

This scheme also necessitated missing my graduation. I mapped out the scenario for Marcia Slothower, who eyed me with skepticism. I could easily tell she did not believe for one minute that Missouri was where the Lord wanted me. But she withheld criticism and said cheerfully, "Well, if it turns out differently, you and Jamie are always welcome to move back in with George and me so you can attend your graduation. It'd be such a shame to miss it."

"Thanks, Marcia," I said, hugging this gracious lady who had become like a mother to me. "But I know it'll work out. Besides," I said, "I gave my dress away."

In those days, Word of Life required all women graduates to wear long gowns. I had been apprised of that prerequisite before I had even enrolled and had brought a gown with me. Now that I saw no need for it, I loaned it to one of the other girls and luxuriated instead in the shelter of knowing what I would be doing come September, when so many others in my class still had no idea. That sure was a load off my mind.

But in no time, the Lord managed to load my mind right back up again. My boss on the island informed me that Jack Wyrtzen wanted me at Word of Life Inn to do, oh yes, the radio broadcast!

"When?" I asked.

"Right now."

Oh no! Here we go again. I began pleading with John. "Can't you get me out of it? I really don't want to do it. Just tell him I can't. Please John, please."

John just laughed. Then when he realized I was serious, he looked at me as though I had lost my mind. "Tell Jack you won't do it? I can't do that! You can't say 'no' to Jack! Just get on a boat and go!"

So I walked down to the dock, boarded a pontoon, and crossed the lake. Scared to death and feeling sick, I trudged up the hill to the Inn, begging the Lord to give me the strength and the words to get through this ordeal. "Why Lord," I kept asking, "are you forcing me to do this? Why?" When we finished, Jack insisted I dine at his table at the Inn that night so I could meet Joan. Joan, I soon discovered, was why.

Joan Steiner Wyrtzen was twenty-five years younger than Jack, just as I had been twenty-five years younger than James. She had been married thirty years when she became a widow, and she was the only friend I had the entire time I was at Word of Life who truly understood how much I missed my husband and how deep was the chasm his death had left in my life. I found myself looking forward to her company, which I was privileged to enjoy primarily on Wednesday nights.

Wednesday was when Jack preached at the campfire on the island. Together they would ride over in Jack's boat, dock it in the boathouse, and stroll past Little Wheels en route to the meeting. Often, however, Jack would go on and Joan would stay behind with me, where we rocked away in our chairs and talked on the comfortable old porch of Little Wheels overlooking Schroon Lake. We talked about the Lord, about our late husbands, about our struggles with widowhood, and our feelings about love and remarriage. Her friendship became a jewel in my life during a difficult, lonely summer. I valued her wisdom, her spiritual maturity, her openness, and her honesty. She was a genuine woman of God whom I admired immensely and whose judgment I trusted implicitly.

Although I never saw myself remarrying, talking to Joan made me wonder if the Lord might have another husband in mind for me someday. I knew Jack felt I should get married again because I had a young child. So I took the matter up with God. I refused to ask for a husband. Instead, I told Him that if it was His will for me to remarry some day, I wanted Him to pick the man out and deliver him right to me.

"If I pick him out Lord," I said, "I'll surely pick the wrong one. If you pick him out, he'll be right. And Lord," I always added, "there are three things I want, if you're doing any picking. First, I want a man who loves you first and foremost—preferably a minister. Second, I want someone who will love me as Christ loves the church and gave His life for it. And third, I want someone who will love my daughter as his own flesh and blood." Every now and then, I would also add, "And Lord, I'd really appreciate it if he has a good sense of humor."

Those were my requests in the exact order I always prayed them. And I never told a single, solitary soul.

Eventually the end of August rolled around. Three more days and the island now pulsing with teenagers would shut down for the long, cold winter. The Bible Institute was getting ready for graduation in four days and I was getting ready for Missouri. My plethora of boxes were neatly stacked and labeled "Child Evangelism Institute, Warrenton, MO." All that remained was for the boat to come by the next day to pick them up and deposit them on the mainland, where they would be shipped to the Midwest. Jamie was duly enrolled in school in Missouri, and I had received my dormitory assignment.

Everything was set. All I needed to ensure my security was word from The Friends of Israel that it wanted me in January. Then I could give my tenants sufficient time to find another place to live, I could move back into my home in New Jersey when I returned from Warrenton, and I would have plenty of time to enroll Jamie in school for January 1987. My ducks were in a row. My life was in order. How good it was to be in control.

Then the boom fell.

As the sun was setting, with less than twelve hours to go before my worldly goods were scheduled for evacuation, I heard from The Friends of Israel. "We can't wait until January. We need you right now."

I turned ashen. To everyone who saw me, I must have looked like the ghost of Christmas past because they all wanted to know what was wrong and why I was so white. Slowly I made my way back to Little Wheels, past my boxes, and into my little room where I sat down, alone and depressed. It was impossible, I thought. There was no way I could go to The Friends of Israel before January. No way. First, I had no place to live in New Jersey. My brother was now in California, so I could not move in with him. My friend Jean had just moved to Ohio. Mrs. Bennett was still in North Carolina, as was most of James's family. What was I supposed to do? Live on the street? Jamie was entering second grade in two weeks, and I wanted her back in private school. Who would take her so late? And with no place to live, how could I even figure out where to try to enroll her?

"Lord," I cried. "How could you do this to me? If you wanted me to go to The Friends of Israel in September, why didn't you just tell me earlier? You know I would've gone. All you had to do was tell me. Why did you do this? What do I do now? What do I do?"

My neat little plan had backfired. Instead of giving me security, it had plunged me into turmoil. The last thing I wanted was to have to make a decision. I had begged the Lord for months not to force me into a decision. "Just tell me what to do," I had pleaded, "and I'll do it. Just don't make me choose."

Jack Wyrtzen had already warned me about that type of praying. It had never worked for him, he said. "Every time I had an open door, I had two, and the Lord made me choose." Now I had two. But how could I discern which door was God's and which was not.

Night had fallen. Jamie was getting ready for bed, and I was sweeping out the little room we had called home when I heard a friendly voice say "Hi!" There was Joan, standing in my doorway. It was Wednesday. "I was on my way to the campfire with Jack," she said, "and the Lord told me to turn around and come back here to you."

I put down my broom, tucked Jamie in, and turned out the light. We walked onto the porch, eased into our chairs, and I spilled my entire dilemma. She listened thoughtfully and we talked.

"Hmmm. I see," she said. "You were called to the Jewish people, weren't you?"

"Yes," I said. That much I knew for certain.

"Why do want to go to CEF, Lorna?"

I thought for a moment. "Because it's such good training." "It's good training for someday."

"Yes," I said. "It's very good training for someday."

"But why are you preparing for 'someday' today? God will prepare you for 'someday' when the time comes."

Soon the campfire ended, Jack stopped by to collect his wife, and we said good night. I entered my room that night and dropped to my knees beside the bed where Jamie was sleeping. "Lord," I said, "maybe my problem is faith. I have none." I had learned during my year at the Bible Institute that the opposite of faith is pride. "Behold, his soul that is lifted up [proud] is not upright in him; but the just shall live by his faith"(Hab. 2:4). Faith means trusting God. Pride means trusting oneself. In the final analysis, who had concocted the grand scheme for my so-called security? Was it God, or was it I?

I knew what I had to do. I opened my Bible to Hebrews 11, that great chapter of faith, and began reading.

> *Now faith is the substance of things hoped for, the evidence of things not seen. For by it the elders received witness. Through faith we understand that the worlds were framed by the word of God, so that things which are seen were not made of things which do appear"* (vv. 1–3).

It continues:

> *But without faith it is impossible to please him [God]; for he that cometh to God must believe that he is, and that he is a rewarder of them that diligently seek him"* (v. 6).

Without faith, it is impossible to please Him. I wanted so much to please God and to be in His perfect will. I stood in the valley of decision and whatever I did, I had to evidence

faith. Did I trust the Lord, or didn't I? Who else was there
to trust if not the Lord? As I stayed on my knees reading
and speaking to Him, the Lord finally lifted His still small
voice; and in His mercy, which endures forever, He spoke
to me:

> By faith Abraham, **when he was called** to go out
> into a place which he should after receive for an
> inheritance, **obeyed; and he went out, not know-
> ing where he went** [emphases added] (Heb. 11:8).

There was my answer. Of the two doors that lay open
before me, only one had been opened by God; and He just
told me which one it was. The Lord had called me to the
Jewish people. That fact was indisputable. Now it was up
to me to obey and to exercise faith in Him, the God of
Abraham, Isaac, and Jacob—even though I did not know
where I was going to live. It was for me to obey and for
Him to provide. I did not have to know how. I did not
have to know the details. All I had to do was trust.

Exercising faith in God, I had learned, often involves
doing the very opposite of what the world tells us to do. The
world says, "Take care of Number One." God says, "Make
me Number One, and I'll take care of you." The world says,
"You are the captain of your ship." God says, "Let me be the
captain of your ship, and I'll steer you straight forever." The
world says, "You've got to trust in yourself and plan your
life." God says, "Trust in me, put your life in my hands, and
I'll make it count for all eternity."

I knew whom I had believed and that He was faithful.
Wasn't it written in the Bible, "my God shall supply all
your need according to his riches in glory by Christ Jesus"
(Phil. 4:19)? My most pressing needs were for a place to
live and a school for Jamie. The God I knew and had trusted through the blood of the Lord Jesus Christ would keep

His promises. Still on my knees, I began to ask the Lord for a verse to confirm His will.

Within minutes I was at Deuteronomy 31:8: "And the LORD, he it is who doth go before thee; he will be with thee, he will not fail thee, neither forsake thee; fear not, neither be dismayed."

My decision was made. I was going to The Friends of Israel. That day will forever remain in my memory. It was August 20, 1986—Jamie's seventh birthday.

What a glorious morning I awoke to. The sun was shining. The birds were singing, and my soul was so filled with the joy of the Lord and excitement over how He would fulfill His promises to me that I couldn't wait to tell everyone I was going home to New Jersey. One of the first people I told was Jamie.

"Guess what?" I said, sitting with her on the pontoon boat as it skimmed across Schroon Lake, bringing us to the mainland for an appointment I had at Word of Life Inn. "We're going home."

"Really?" she said.

After the boat ferried us to the mainland, we disembarked and began walking up the slope from the dock to Route 9. "Now I'm going to be able to go to my graduation," I told her. "You're going to get to see Mommy graduate." That thought certainly did not do as much for her as it did for me. But it did jog her memory. As we held hands making our way to the road, it dawned on her that I had given away my dress.

"But Mommy," she said looking up at me, her curls bouncing in the sunlight. "What are you going to wear for a dress?"

"I don't know, honey," I replied. "But you know what? If God wants me in the graduation, He'll provide a dress."

At that moment, we reached the road. Just as we were getting ready to cross the street and walk up the hill to the Inn, two people in a little pickup truck started waving furiously and tooting their horn. It was Todd and Linda, married students whom I had not seen since classes had ended in May. They had returned home to Maine to do their summer ministry and were driving through Schroon Lake en route to Piedmont Bible College in North Carolina where Todd was going to study missionary aviation. They pulled over to the side of the road and we embraced. How wonderful it was to see them again and to trade stories of how God was leading in our lives.

I told them what He had just done for me. "And now I can even go to the graduation," I laughed, "and I don't have a dress." Suddenly Linda's eyes grew bright with excitement. "Lorna," she said. "I have a dress you can wear."

"Right. What is it, a size two?" Linda was a petite little thing, and diminutiveness was never my claim to fame.

"No," she said. "Not *my* dress. The dress my mother wore to my wedding. I told her I didn't need it, but at the last minute she insisted I put it in the truck." It was not even packed. Linda walked over to the truck, flipped up the tarpaulin covering the contents on the flatbed, and right there on top—lying neatly over all the boxes and suitcases and still on the coat hanger—was a beautiful, long gown in exactly the color I would have bought for myself and in exactly my size. "Oh, the depth of the riches both of the wisdom and knowledge of God! How unsearchable are his judgments, and his ways past finding out!" (Rom. 11:33).

Not ten minutes after my daughter had asked, "What are you going to wear for a dress?" God had provided it. What wonderful confirmation that I had made the right decision. With a profound peace and a joy I could hardly contain, I draped the dress over my arm and walked with Jamie to Word of Life Inn to keep my appointment.

If only the world understood how personally God intervenes in the daily affairs of men and how much He delights in helping those who have placed their faith in Him. I could not help but remember the story my mother-in-law had told me about the little girl who had asked the Lord Jesus for a pair of red shoes. She knew in whom she had believed, and had come to Him in the confidence of His great love. Why would anyone reject such a marvelous One as He?

That afternoon I called Marcia Slothower and told her my news. She was ecstatic. The next day Jamie and I moved off the island and back to the Slothowers' home. As the pontoon carried me to the mainland for the last time over the familiar waters of Schroon Lake, I looked behind me to the white boathouse fading in the distance. I began to cry. What a special place Word of Life had been for me that year, and what a very special work God had done in my heart. As the boathouse grew smaller and smaller, I thanked Him over and over for having given me the opportunity to dedicate one year of my life exclusively to studying the Word of God, so He could change my life forever.

Chapter Seven

The Road Home

The year was 1938. The world differed little from what it is today. Violence and hatred, Satan's unchanging bedfellows, comfortably roamed the earth; and murder, now called "ethnic cleansing," had ascended to top priority on Germany's bureaucratic list of things to do. All of Europe would soon be embroiled in a fight for its life against a despot named Adolph Hitler, whose sick obsession it was to rid the world of Jews.

Across the ocean in Philadelphia, Pennsylvania, the Lord was moving in the hearts of a group of godly men and women whose love for the Jewish people was exceeded only by their love for the Jewish Savior. In an effort to aid God's Chosen People, they formed The Friends of Israel Gospel Ministry and Relief Society, with a primary goal of providing much-needed food, medical supplies, clothing, and housing—in the name of Jesus Christ—to Jewish people fleeing Europe. The organization also taught Bible in an effort to communicate the love of Christ and to dispel the erroneous notion that Hitler and the Nazis were Christians.

Over the years The Friends of Israel has grown into a sound, Bible-centered ministry committed to evangelism, education, and edification. It holds fast to the Word of God as the only beacon of truth in a dark, corrupted world; and it makes no apologies for teaching that the land of Israel belongs to the Jewish people forever, that God has a glorious future for Israel, and that Jesus is the promised Messiah.

Today The Friends of Israel is one of the world's premiere Bible-teaching organizations. Its highly acclaimed, bimonthly magazine, *Israel My Glory*, is read by a quarter of a million people around the globe, and its books and resource materials are now being translated into other languages. We have workers on five continents, a free medical clinic in Argentina, and our transglobal radio broadcast, where the news is always the good news of the Messiah, reaches millions.

Of course, I knew none of this when I checked in with The Friends of Israel in September 1986. In His usually miraculous way, the Lord provided abundantly for me. Over the next six weeks, I hauled Jamie and the contents of a single suitcase between the houses of three terrific friends, one week here, one week there, until we finally were able to move back home. Unbelievably, I loved those days. They proved a time of joyous blessing that I will never forget.

Since I knew I would be living in Ewing, an hour north of the office, I enrolled Jamie at Bethel Baptist Christian School in Cherry Hill so she would be near me in case of emergency. Then I started work. I had been hired as an editor, but I quickly discovered that no one had anything for me to edit. So I was shepherded into the Data Entry Department and placed under the tutelage of a warm and wonderful woman named Vera, whose duty it was to teach me the computer system and how to handle the volumes of incoming mail. Even today, every piece of mail received at The Friends of Israel is opened by hand. Each letter is read, answered when appropriate; and all prayer requests are prayed over.

Everyone was kind, considerate, and friendly. But I missed Word of Life, and I particularly missed Jack and Joan. Within weeks a letter arrived from Jack, telling me he and Joan were praying for me every day and wanted Jamie and me to come to Schroon Lake to stay with them over Thanksgiving. I declined the invitation since I already had plans to visit my mother-in-law in North Carolina, but how I thanked God for it. It provided a sense of stability and continuity at a time when I sorely needed it.

Meanwhile, the Lord had begun forging a strong relationship between Vera and me. Around noon each day, we would go to lunch and talk. She was only slightly older than Joan, and I soon learned that she had been widowed in her early twenties and had been left with a four-year-old son. Did God know how to put people together or what! Some years later she had remarried, had given birth to another son, and was, so to speak, living happily ever after. Like Joan, she understood the hurt of widowhood and demonstrated enormous compassion for Jamie and me.

She also had a good second marriage. Vera talked a lot about her husband (whom she adored) and a lot about her younger son, who was attending Philadelphia College of Bible (PCB) at the time. But the person she unquestionably talked about the most was her older son, a man named Tom Simcox. In fact, it seemed that the longer I knew her, the more she told me about him.

I learned how Tom had tried to hide from the Lord after God had called him to preach. I learned how the Lord finally had to break him so He could then remold him for His service. I learned how Tom had eventually resumed his college education at the age of twenty-seven—against his mother's advice—with hardly a nickel for tuition or a dime in his pocket, and how he had worked and scrimped and graduated from PCB debt free.

"I was wrong," she said. "I told him he had no business going back to school because he had no money. He told me he had faith. He said the Lord wanted him at PCB, and the Lord was able to pay for it. Tom was right," she said. "I was wrong."

Vera also told me how much her son, a Gentile, loved the Jewish people. It was Tom, in fact, who had gotten her the job at The Friends of Israel. "All he wants to do," she said, "is teach Jewish people the Bible through The Friends of Israel." She also imparted one more critical piece of information. He was—surprise, surprise—single.

Oh-h-h-h No! The last thing I needed at that point was one more complication. My house was a wreck—boxes everywhere. I had a new job, a new school for my daughter, and an hour-long commute twice a day that left little time for socializing.

Little did I suspect that whenever Vera saw Tom, she bent his ear about me. Not that it did any good. Tom, a resolutely independent thinker, had elevated the technique of selective deafness to an art form. When it came to his mother, he only listened to half of what she ever said; and when it came to women, his rule of thumb was simple: "If my mother liked her, I didn't." He wanted nothing to do with me. Case closed.

Tom had also grown weary praying for a wife. He had specific, nonnegotiable requirements that no one seemed to fit. Chief of them all was a love for the Jewish people. "I had given up," he said. "I'd decided I'd probably stay single forever. Every time I'd meet a girl I thought might be a prospective wife, I'd test her out, so to speak, by taking her to a Friends of Israel function. I'd explain the work of The Friends of Israel, and then I'd say, 'This is what I want to do for the rest of my life.' She'd take off and I'd never see her again."

One of Friends of Israel's biggest functions took place Saturday, October 18, when we dedicated the building that now houses our international headquarters. Thousands of people swarmed in and out of the big tents we had erected for the meeting. During a lull in my responsibilities in the tents, Vera pulled me over to introduce me to Tom, who was equally occupied with his duties inside the nearly completed headquarters. We met. We shook hands. We exchanged ten words. We said goodbye.

Monday I was back at work. "You know," Vera said to me as we began opening mail, "My son must've really liked you. He asked me to ask you if you'd be interested in someone who loves the Lord and wants to go into the ministry, who would love you as Christ loves the church and gave His life for it, who would love your daughter as his own flesh and blood, and who loves the Jewish people."

If the shock in my heart made its way to my face, Vera never let on. I had never revealed to a single, human soul what I had prayed. Yet through his mother, Tom had repeated my very words back to me in the exact order in which I had uttered them to the Lord. Well, if Tom wanted to ask me out, that was my sign to say yes.

Ask he did. And the third time we met, he asked me to marry him. Another monumental decision! Few things, I have discovered, drive people to their knees faster than the desperate necessity for God's wisdom in making potentially life-altering decisions. By now I knew that a leap from widow to wife was not without its pitfalls.

God has a very special place in His heart for widows. Several years earlier I had attended a seminar at the Philadelphia Civic Center that made it clear what a privileged position a widow enjoys in God's economy.

The scenario went something like this. According to the Word of God, the husband is the head of the home. As such, he spreads his "umbrella of protection" over his family members, and they stand under it and benefit from its shelter. The Lord also has an umbrella. His is spread over the husband. As the Lord works through the husband, giving him the wisdom and discernment he needs to protect and care for his family, the family enjoys the benefits that come from the hand of God. Of course, the godlier the husband, the sturdier his umbrella.

Unfortunately, no man is perfect. Every husband's umbrella is bound to contain holes. How many holes it has depends entirely on how closely the husband walks with the Lord. Whereas one man's umbrella could be a mighty shelter, another's could leak like a sieve.

The important thing, I was told, is to remain under the umbrella no matter what, because as ventilated as it may be, outside its protection there is no canopy at all; and the family becomes far more vulnerable to evil. What do you do then, if you are a wife who finds yourself stuck under a leaky umbrella? The godly woman prays to the Lord and asks Him to patch the holes, which He does by going to work on the husband. The husband, however, being human, often does not appreciate the patching process, thus forcing the Lord to exert more and more pressure on him—a procedure that often makes things worse before they finally get better.

Widows, though, are special. They have no husband. As a result, they stand directly underneath the protection of God Himself, and *His* umbrella **never** leaks. It is perfect.

For four years I had been privileged to stand directly under God's umbrella. Despite the pain and loneliness, the Lord had radiated His blessings upon me in a million discernible ways. And I had learned that if I leaned wholly on Him, He would clearly direct my path. Never once had He failed me. The last thing I wanted to do now was exchange my special treatment at the hands of the Almighty for a mere arm of flesh. What would happen if I remarried? Jamie and I could be stuck under some leaky umbrella getting soaked.

So I prayed and prayed and prayed. Tom had all the qualities I valued in a husband, and I could see that he clearly adored Jamie. He loved the Jewish people. He had an astounding grasp of the Word of God, which I admired and trusted. He was a man of principle and sound judgment who was not afraid to stand up for what he believed. When it came to the things of the Lord, we were so in tune that we seemed like one mind in two bodies. And if all that were not enough, he even had a wonderful sense of humor.

Yes, the time had come to get married again, and Tom was the man. Now I would have to relinquish my position as head of my home and willingly stand under Tom's umbrella. It would be the beginning of yet another journey of faith, one in which I would have to learn how to pray for my husband and to trust God to direct his footsteps.

It didn't take long before news of my engagement made it up to Word of Life. The next thing I knew, Jack Wyrtzen was on the telephone with The Friends of Israel, investigating my husband-to-be.

"Who is this Tom Simcox?" Jack asked. "Does he love the Lord? Will he be a good husband to Lorna and a good father to Jamie?" When Jack was assured that Tom met all the necessary criteria, he gave his blessing. We were married several months later.

Two weeks later we went up to Word of Life to take Jamie to snow camp. While Jamie bunked down at the Bible Institute dormitory, we were the guests of George and Marcia Slothower. They were so happy for me and welcomed Tom the minute they saw him. The next morning, as we relaxed and enjoyed the view from the big picture windows overlooking the frozen expanse of Schroon Lake, I heard a big, booming voice at the front door.

"Where are the newlyweds!" It was Jack and Joan. Swaddled in wrapping paper was a wedding present that Joan had commissioned for us. It was a beautiful watercolor that bore the immortal words of the Lord from Jeremiah 29:11: "For I know the plans that I have for you, declares the LORD, plans for welfare and not for calamity to give you a future and a hope" (NASB).

"It's the verse we chose for our marriage," she said. "We have it hanging in our bedroom, and we wanted to give the same thing to you." It hangs today in our living room as a testimony to the goodness and love of God, whose mercies are new every morning. Ten months later the Lord blessed us with another beautiful daughter, Andrea Noel.

For the next nine years, Jack or Joan wrote to us; and often Jack called us at home just to see how we were doing or to invite us to stay at the Word of Life Inn for a week as his guests. When we would get up there, he always found time to take us out on the lake in his wonderful old boat with the red leather seats. Joan would grill hamburgers and hot dogs, and we would sit on the patio and talk. What a gift those days were.

When Jack discovered that Tom had still never seen Word of Life Island, he immediately piled us all into his boat, ferried us over, and gave Tom the grand tour himself, making sure to include all the marvelous stories of workmen who got saved while installing pipes or waterlines. One of Jack's greatest joys was to proclaim how God had changed a life.

The last time I spoke to Jack was early in 1996. I was cooking and the telephone rang. The voice was unmistakable. He just wanted to know how we were doing. "You know Jack," I told him, "my father died when I was in college. The Lord always seemed to provide a mother figure for me, but I never really had anyone look out for me like a father until you came along. You've been a lot like a dad to me."

"Well," he said, "we all have spiritual fathers, don't we." The amazing thing about Jack Wyrtzen, though, was that he treated so many others just as he treated me.

I continued to stay close to Mrs. Bennett, who was getting on in years. But the same sweet spirit and love of Christ shone brightly in her life. She now suffered from a multiplicity of ailments, but never complained. At least once a year we drove down to see her, and she graciously put us all up at her home, even though I knew it was difficult for her to see me with someone other than James.

In the summer of 1992, just weeks before her ninetieth birthday, she took a bad fall at her home and broke her hip. After undergoing surgery, she remained in the hospital, where she was recovering beautifully when her lungs began to fill with fluid. The more congested her lungs became, the more labored her breathing grew. She asked the doctors to increase her flow of oxygen, but they said there was nothing further they could do.

"I'm ready to go then," she said, barely able to breathe. "God is so good." Shortly thereafter, she closed her eyes for the last time and was in the presence of her beloved Lord.

She had come close to death one other time that I remember, a number of years earlier. I will never forget the story she told me concerning that incident. "I looked up," she said, "and I saw an angel. He was going to take me into heaven, and He asked me who the person was I most wanted to see."

That's easy, I thought to myself. If someone had asked me, I would have said James. She probably said Barney, her husband who had been dead almost forty years. "What did you tell him?" I asked.

She looked at me almost quizzically, wondering how I could have asked such a ridiculous question. In a clear, matter-of-fact voice, she replied simply, "Why, I told him 'I want to see the Lord and thank Him for saving me.'" That was Thelma Bennett. She died as she had lived—with the praise of God on her lips and the love of Christ in her heart.

On April 17, 1996, Jack Wyrtzen followed her into the presence of the Almighty; and on May 23, 1997, Marcia

Slothower arrived there also. Eventually, praise God, I will join them. And as Eugene M. Bartlett Sr. wrote, "some sweet day I'll sing up there the song of victory."

One of my favorite hymns—I know them now—is *Victory in Jesus*, penned by Bartlett in the 1930s. I used to sing it to Jamie when she was six years old as we held hands and tromped together through the knee-deep snow in Schroon Lake. It goes like this:

I heard an old, old story,
how a Savior came from glory,
How He gave His life on Calvary
to save a wretch like me;
I heard about His groaning,
of His precious blood's atoning,
Then I repented of my sins and won the victory.

O victory in Jesus, my Savior, forever!
He sought me and bought me
with His redeeming blood;
He loved me ere I knew Him,
and all my love is due Him—
He plunged me to victory
beneath the cleansing flood.

How I praise God for that victory and for the home in heaven He has made for me forever. God is indeed faithful. And He has promised, through that great saint Jeremiah, "ye shall seek me, and find me, when ye shall search for me with all your heart" (Jer. 29:13).

Amid all the lies and all the fantasies that have been so intricately woven into the fabric of life—the truth is still there, waiting to be found. It is there for anyone who comes to God for the answers. The Bible says that all mankind is lost in sin and shame. So was I when I started searching for the truth. Yet in the end, it was Jesus, the everlasting God of my people Israel, that Great Shepherd of the sheep and lover of our souls, who, in His infinite mercy and grace, had come searching for me.

My friend Joan Wyrtzen told me that God has a wonderful way of rearranging our lives. She once heard it described this way: It's as though you had your camera set to take a picture. You focused on your subject and were just about to snap the shutter when God took the camera from your hand, changed all your settings, refocused your lens on a completely different subject, snapped the picture for you, and it was exactly what you had wanted all along.

When I joined The Friends of Israel, I was alone—a widow and single parent with a daughter in second grade—and I never did get the editing job I had been promised. Instead, God took my camera and pointed it at an entirely different subject. He gave me a wonderful husband, a family of in-laws who love me as a daughter and love my daughter as their own, another beautiful girl, and enabled me to teach others the truth I had so desperately sought for myself. Click!

Then thirteen years later, God took my camera again, refocused it, and gave me the type of job I had loved and had been equipped to do in the first place. In 1999 I was named senior editor for The Friends of Israel. Click! And both pictures turned out to be exactly what I had wanted!

I do not know what the future holds, but "I know whom I have believed and am persuaded that he is able to keep that which I have committed unto him against that day" (2 Tim. 1:12). And when the day comes when my sojourn on this earth is over, He'll take my camera yet again—and point it home.

MORE BOOKS FROM THE FRIENDS OF ISRAEL

by Elwood McQuaid
Executive Director

THE ZION CONNECTON
Elwood McQuaid takes a thoughtful, sensitive look at relations between Jewish people and evangelical Christians, including the controversial issues of anti-Semitism, the rise of Islam, the right of Jewry to a homeland in the Middle East, and whether Christians should try to reach Jewish people with the gospel message—and how.
ISBN 0-915540-40-1, #B61, $9.95

II PETER: STANDING FAST IN THE LAST DAYS
- How can we live for God during these climatic days before the Lord returns?
- How can we identify false teachers and charlatans?
- How can we understand what eternity holds?

This excellent volume provides answers to these important questions from the little but powerful Bible book of 2 Peter. Its timely message will become an invaluable addition to your life as well as your personal library.
ISBN 0-915540-65-7, #B79, $10.95

ZVI: THE MIRACULOUS STORY OF TRIUMPH OVER THE HOLOCAUST

For more than half a century, *ZVI* has endured as the best-selling book produced by the ministry of The Friends of Israel. Millions of people have been touched, inspired, and encouraged by this story of a World War II waif in Warsaw, Poland, and how he found his way to Israel and faith in the Messiah. Now *ZVI* and its sequel, *ZVI and the Next Generation*, are combined in this new release. The whole story—together at last. It is a book you will find difficult to lay down.
ISBN 0-915540-66-5, #B80, $11.95

by David M. Levy
Director of Foreign Ministries

THE TABERNACLE: SHADOWS OF THE MESSIAH

This superb work on Israel's wilderness Tabernacle explores in depth the service of the priesthood and the significance of the sacrifices. The well-organized content and numerous illustraions will open new vistas of biblical truth as ceremonies, sacrifices, and priestly service reveal the perfections of the Messiah
ISBN 0-915540-17-7, #B51, $9.95

REVELATION: HEARING THE LAST WORD

Why is there so much uncertainty and disagreement about the last days? What can we know about the Antichrist? In what order will the events of the last days take place? What will happen to Israel during the Tribulation? What will life be like during the Millennial Kingdom? This valuable resource will help you know what we can expect as we approach earth's final hour
ISBN 0-915540-60-6, #B75, $11.95

GUARDING THE GOSPEL OF GRACE

We often lack peace, joy, or victory in our walk with Christ because we're not clear how God's grace works in our lives. The books of Galatians and Jude are brought together in this marvelous work that explains grace and what can happen if you stray from it. Don't miss out on the difference that God's grace can make in your life . . . It's nothing less than amazing!

ISBN 0-915540-26-6, #B67, $9.95

by Renald E. Showers
National Ministries Representative

MARANATHA: OUR LORD, COME!

A Definitive Study of the Rapture of the Church

Here is an in-depth study of matters related to the Rapture of the church. It addresses such issues as the birth-pang concept in the Bible and ancient Judaism, the biblical concept of the Day of the Lord, the relationship of the Day of the Lord to the Time of Jacob's Trouble and the Great Tribulation, the identification of the sealed scroll of Revelation 5, the significance of the seals, the imminent coming of Christ with His holy angels, the relationship of church saints to the wrath of God, the significance of 2 Thessalonians 2, the implications of both the 70-week prophecy of Daniel 9 and the references to Israel and the church in the book of the Revelation, the meaning of the last trump, and why the timing of the Rapture has practical implications for daily living and ministry.

ISBN 0-915540-22-3 #B55p, $10.95

THERE REALLY IS A DIFFERENCE!

A Comparison of Covenant and Dispensational Theology
Should you attend a church that teaches Covenant Theology or one that teaches Dispensational Theology? Is there a difference between the two? Yes, there is. This excellent volume will explain what these differences are and how they affect issues such as God's ultimate purpose for history, God's program for Israel, the nature and beginning of the church, and the Christian's relationship to the Mosaic Law and grace. It also explores the differences between the premillennial, amillennial, and postmillennial views of the Kingdom of God and presents and apology for the dispensational-premillennial system of theology.
ISBN 0-915540-50-9, #B36, $9.95

THOSE INVISIBLE SPIRITS CALLED ANGELS

Everywhere we look, angels are in the spotlight—on prime-time TV, in bestselling books, and on the shelves of well-known gift stores. More and more people report fascinating encounters with angels. But very little of what we're hearing these days matches what the Bible says about angels. And the Bible has a lot to say about who angels are, what they do, and how they minister to us. You'll discover all that and much more in this excellent and easy-to-read volume by Dr. Showers.
ISBN 0-915540-24-X, #B66, $9.95

by Steve Herzig
Director of North American Ministries

JEWISH CULTURE & CUSTOMS
A Sampler of Jewish Life
Every area of Jewish life radiates with rich symbolism and special meaning. From meals, clothing, and figures of speech to worship, holidays, and weddings, we find hundreds of fascinating traditions that date as far back as two or three thousand years. How did these customs get started? What special meaning do they hold? And what can they teach us? Explore the answers to these questions in this enjoyable sampler of the colorful world of Judaism and Jewish life. You'll gain a greater appreciation for God's Chosen People and see key aspects of the Bible and Christianity in a whole new light.
ISBN 0-915540-31-2, #B68, $8.95

by Bruce Scott
Ministry Representative

THE FEASTS OF ISRAEL
Seasons of the Messiah
Many of the Bible's most incredible prophecies about Christ are intricately hidden within the Jewish holidays and feasts of the Old Testament. That's where you'll find little-known yet astounding pictures of Christ's deity, His death and resurrection, and even His Second Coming and future reign as King of kings and Lord of lords. You'll discover that much of what Jesus said and did—which seems mysterious to us today—suddenly makes complete sense. Don't miss any part of the greatest story ever told.
ISBN 0-915540-14-2, #B65, $9.95